She DID IT AND SO CAN You

17 Inspirational Women SHARE THEIR STORIES & STEPS OF HOW THEY ACHIEVED Rapid Success

By Empowered Women Publishing

She Did It!

Disclaimer:

All the information, techniques, skills, and concepts contained within this publication are of the nature of general comment only and are not in any way recommended as individual advice. The intent is to offer a variety of information to provide a wider range of choices now and in the future, recognising that we all have widely diverse circumstances and viewpoints. Should any reader choose to make use of the information contained herein, this is their decision and the author and publishers do not assume any responsibilities whatsoever under any condition or circumstances.

Foreword

Have you ever wondered how *She Did It*? And if you could do it too? Recent years have made more women stop and question what is really serving them in life. They've made us wonder how we can pivot and break the patterns holding us back. But how do you go from where you are now to the life you desire? What actions do you have to take today to get there?

In *She Did It* you'll discover how 17 women from around the world created rapid success in their lives and business. You'll learn how they overcame their fear and blocks and what actions they took to break through it all and change everything.

Not only will you get to know 17 incredible and inspirational stories, but you'll also get to learn from them. In each chapter, they'll share a few steps you can implement in your own life or business TODAY – not in months or years from now!

This book will show you that it's possible to change your life or start a business from scratch and create rapid success in both. You'll discover how the women in this book are no different to you - they were also afraid and had blocks to overcome at times as well.

The following stories you're about to read have proven results and each chapter provides secrets that will help you create rapid success in your life and business. Each woman has a different story, different challenges to overcome and achieved different successes.

Just remember that success is available to all.

She Did It! ...and so can you!

Contents

Alisha Whaley

Where it all started

How do you know when you've made it? How do you determine if you are a success? How would you even *define* "success"?

I've lived most of my life under the assumption that the term *"success"* referred to individuals with some form of expertise. In other words, people who excelled at business, acting, or were musically talented. Because of these thoughts, I viewed myself as just an average human without a great talent so therefore I couldn't define success for myself. Sure, I was skilled at being a wife, mom of twins and a graphic designer - I was even a decent photographer - but with less than 600 followers on Instagram and a whopping 30 subscribers on my email list, I was absolutely not an expert in anything. Homeschooled until 10th grade, with my GED at the age of 16, a graphic arts certificate at 19, a marriage at 21 and twins at the age of 24, I was a nobody, from a small town very few have heard of, even those who live in the close cities.

Basically, I'd spent my entire life thinking that I was too average to be labeled a *"success"*. I didn't have a major life event that changed me forever; didn't have the advantage of a brain that never stopped or a type A personality. I lived with the inner dialogue of *"you are a nobody."* Yep. A totally average nobody.

This narrative floated around in my head for years and by the end of 2019, I dug myself into a rut so deep that I became numb. I didn't care about the holidays and I didn't want to be around my family. I was depressed and burnt out on life so when 2020 started, I knew something had to change. I was determined to never feel that level of burnout ever again but there was one problem - I didn't know where to even start. I had no clue how to pull myself out of that rut. I just knew that I had to do it myself.

If you had told me at the beginning of 2020 before all the drama happened that I would be starting the following year with triple the revenue I made during a pandemic and be a published author alongside other incredible women AND would be well on my way to making over $100k in my business, I'd have told you that you were the definition of insane.

Looking back through all I have learned, I can see the point where it all changed though, at the time, I was terrified and uncertain that I could ever find a way through the noise. It started with a dream and took a boatload of courage but I rose to new levels of *"success"* through simplifying everything. I am beyond grateful for the anxiety-riddled lessons and the late nights I spent lying awake, worrying about how to find the clients to pay my expenses. I'm grateful for the journey because, without it, I wouldn't be here in this book telling you that I did it! I know how to define what success means because I made it and I know for a fact that YOU can too!

I am first and foremost a mom. Mom-life takes up about 90 percent of my time. My passion and mission in life is to help other mompreneurs and women who are building online empires. I want to provide the tools to dream BIGGER, find the COURAGE to take imperfect action and RISE to new levels of success, over and over. Helping others realize their potential and say *"HECK YES! I AM an expert in my industry!"*.

Generating a "success" mindset

Success for me is not giving up. It's taking action even when you don't know what's on the other side. Success is saying, *"I'll figure it out"*.

I pride myself on being able to dig deep and asking loads of questions that help you to brain dump your wildest dreams. I am wicked-good at decoding those dreams and simplifying them. At reordering the dreams into bit sized action steps. Because - let's face it - it's mega overwhelming to be in the middle of mom life, raising the next generation while simultaneously trying to build a business empire online. I know because I live it. Having someone who can decode your thoughts is freedom. Freedom to be less stressed at home; freedom to spend more time doing what makes you happiest because, at the end of the day, it's not about being an expert or having an overabundance of followers. It's not even about the revenue. It's about freedom and what that does for your lifestyle.

It all starts with your mindset. Shifting the focus, like I did, from *"I'll never be good enough"* to *"heck yes I'm good enough, and I'll figure it out!"*. Here's the thing, though. Nothing will take your lifestyle or your business farther than being true to yourself. Knowing who you are under and embracing that woman with open arms. Telling her it's safe to come out and shine. The world has been waiting for her to show up as nothing more than herself.

Unconditionally, unapologetically and authentically you.

Nothing less.

I had no idea how to do any of that in the beginning. I didn't even know that entrepreneurship was even a thing. I thought that was a term reserved for rich people on TV but at the very mature age of 6 years old, I knew that I wanted to impact my small world and made it a point to tell my Dad that, often. He would always laugh and ask me what I wanted to do. I never had an answer for him other than... *"well, I don't want to be famous, but I do want to make a difference. I want to impact someone's life. Help them somehow"*. That's about as much explanation as I could come up with at the time. Years later when I was graduating from the Graphics Arts program, I told my mom that I had no intention of getting a job as a graphic designer or working in a cubicle. She laughed and asked, *"Okay, then what are you going to do?"*. I had the same answer. I didn't know. I just knew that I still felt called to make an impact, but now that I was technically an adult, I

5

also knew I needed an income. So, whilst I was figuring out my future, I got a job in the printing department of OfficeMax and ended up designing brochures, business cards, menus and the like for customers who needed things created and then printed.

Looking back, OfficeMax was the launch pad for everything that came after. Not long after I started working in the print department, a customer (who was a regular) asked if I would be interested in continuing to design for her but as her part time assistant. I jumped at the chance.

I learned a great deal from that experience. She was an entrepreneur herself and introduced me to the possibilities of what being an entrepreneur offered. I was hooked. That is, until I got married and my husband had to travel. He asked me to quit and travel with him and, of course, I couldn't say no. I still wasn't sure that I wanted to be a graphic designer and took the time on the road to try new things. I attempted making jewelry, but quickly found it was tedious and not for me. Then my husband gifted me my first DSLR and I fell in love with photography. For a whole year, I pursued becoming a portrait/wedding photographer. I adored taking photos of brides and helping them remember the beauty of their special day. I still did graphics on the side occasionally but photography had been in the back of my mind since I was a young adult and I was determined to make it a thing. That is, until I got pregnant with twins and life came to a screeching halt. My husband and I decided that I would be at stay-home mom. It didn't pan out to have me work when most of my income would be going on childcare anyway.

Following the birth of our twin boys, my husband launched his own company and was back to working 80+ hours a week and traveling for weeks on end, only this time, I couldn't go with him.

Being home with our boys was a blessing and a curse. I was (and still am) tremendously grateful for having the option to stay home, but I was lonely. I needed an outlet. I spent most of my time in the world of little kids and quickly became depressed, losing my sense of self. This was a pivotal moment for me. I had massive mom guilt. I woke up and went to bed thinking about getting back into graphic design. I still had no idea I could be an entrepreneur but I had to do something.

I was so deep into survival mode in the early years of my boys' lives that to this day, I can't remember how I got started pursuing website design. I had been dabbling in designing websites and logos for a few years when my boys started kindergarten and I suddenly had hours of free time every day. I remember thinking one day, *"hmmm, maybe I could make this a real thing"*. I had no idea how to move forward so I went in search of answers and discovered a Facebook ad for a free five day workshop that claimed to have all the answers I was looking for. I quickly signed up. I couldn't wait to learn all the things.

That was the catalyst to where I am today. The workshop was one of the very first that Kelly Roach did for her signature LIVE Launch Method, at the end of the workshop she was giving one of the viewers a 30 minute one-on-one call with herself. Somehow, I ended up being the lucky person that got to speak with Kelly directly. I was sitting in my car, parked at a small convenience store with my friend's three- year-old in the back seat. Sitting there pouring out my struggles to Kelly, my world as I knew it changed forever. That day was the first step I took in a very long journey towards becoming my own boss. I joined her coaching program not knowing that I would be about to learn one of the hardest lessons in my career. I told Kelly that I would have to move slowly in building my business because my boys were still little and we were currently selling one house, moving and building another home. She assured me that going slow was okay.

That was the first of many lessons I learned.

It's okay to move slowly. Greatness isn't built overnight. It takes a lot of trial and error. It takes many pivots and focal shifts. The only thing that will prevent you from making it to that distant goal or dream is simply [not] taking some type of action. I knew this deep in my gut. This knowledge is what led me to say yes to a design project that turned out to be not only a giant mistake but also another cross road I had to navigate. I had taken on a rush project that required some website design and funnel build-out. I had never done a funnel before but was eager to take on the challenge. Everything that could go wrong did. I had massive anxiety and stress over the whole thing. I knew if the tables were turned, I would SO not be happy with the results and knew that I needed to own up to my mistake. In that moment ,I developed the first core value of my business.

Honesty.

Even though I knew I was good at graphic design, I had no idea how to navigate the technical side of a website. I could make it look mega pretty, but that's where my skill set ended. Honesty became the driving force behind everything that has come after. Not just being upfront with potential clients and telling them specifically what I can and cannot do, but more so, being honest with myself. Holding myself accountable and staying true to who I am as an individual. This was a super hard concept for me to implement though. I had spent most of my life telling myself that I wasn't an expert and would never be at expert level. Having to tell this client that I had made a major mistake and was not the right designer for her needs was crushing. I spiraled. Hard.

I started to doubt everything. My ability to be an entrepreneur; my ability to take care of the house and be a good wife and mom. I battled feeling like I would never be able to do what I saw so many other women doing. I would never be able to live life on my terms because I lacked the knowledge of how to troubleshoot the technical aspects of a website. I didn't know how to code. I had no desire to learn. Why I used my lack of technical skills as an excuse to go back to feeling inadequate on all fronts, I've no idea. But I went back to feeling guilt all the time. Guilty for being on the computer, designing, instead of vacuuming. I felt guilty for wishing I could just go create graphics instead of doing the laundry. I was a mess. I thought about quitting daily. About giving up on my dream of having a branding empire. But every time I would go to quit, something would keep me from doing so. I'd get another client or everyone and their dog would tell me I couldn't and that I was too talented to not stick with it. I would just think "Yah, sure, talent alone won't get you far". Clearly I needed to change my focus. I just didn't know where to start.

Even though I was in this coaching program, I still felt stuck. I couldn't find a way forward. Graphics were all I knew, but I was tired of hustling. I was tired of posting on social media, tired of creating content, tired of feeling like I was working super hard and getting nowhere. I did everything the experts said to grow an audience; to convert followers into buyers, yet none of it was working and I couldn't figure out why.

Queue the wanting to quit. Again.

The Steps

That's when it hit me. I mentored a lot of friends, family and clients. I told them how to create epic graphics and how to get unstuck but not once had I ever taken my own advice. Not once did I turn my talents and skills on myself. So, I decided to take a step back and look at everything I was doing from the perspective of "if I were to mentor myself, what would I say and do to help myself get unstuck".

The first thing I did was to invest in a mindset coach who turned out to be an enneagram expert. She taught me what my number was and how my personality reacts to certain situations. As a 9, I tend to hide my true self in fear of potential conflict. The biggest breakthrough was in learning that I lived in constant conflict with myself. That whole feeling guilty for doing anything graphics related AND feeling guilt for wanting to do graphics instead of house chores? That was the conflict that fueled everything else. One of the things I did to help me be more resilient to this form of conflict was, instead of making a list of things I needed to accomplish in a day, I would ONLY write down a task I had completed. By the end of the day, I realized, I did a heck of a lot and needed to let go of this idea that life could fit into a perfectly curated box.

This one simple ritual led me back to my core value of honesty. I dug deep and asked myself loads of questions, each one pulled out of my wildest dreams. That's when I discovered I had an immense fear of succeeding. I was terrified of being a success and the conflicts that might be triggered with my closest friends and family. Breaking free from this wasn't easy and to be honest, I still have to implement several of the steps I used to break through the fears, daily. Whenever I feel myself sinking, getting overwhelmed, or starting to reach burn out, I turn to my list of steps and do at least 3 of the 6:

1. Start my day with a cup of coffee and journal 3-5 gratitudes
2. End the day by write out a list of the tasks I have completed
3. Take a hot bath and read a fictional book
4. Go to bed at a time that ensures I get a full 8 hours of sleep
5. Meditate on opening myself up to receive the success I desire
6. Spend 24hrs doing something entirely random and unscheduled

Throughout my journey of being a wife, mother and now entrepreneur I see now that it was the fear of succeeding that held me back. Breaking free from feeling like you just don't have what it takes to be great is just plain hard. Yet, if you are willing to take the first step, the freedom that comes with shedding all those self doubts, it's energizing.

Since I can't ask you in person, I want to leave you with a little advice. Go find your center. Who you are under all the masks and the labels. Discover who you are at your core.

Figure out your enneagram number and then go learn your Human Design chart. Those two resources have made the biggest impact on my life. Knowing who you are at your core will unlock everything else. It's not about the hustle. It's not about the follower count. It's not even about your skill set. Your deepest desires are possible and can be achieved by first embracing your raw unapologetic self and then unleashing that person on the world. There is only one YOU on this planet. Only YOU have experienced life in the way that you have and because of that, the world needs your voice and your talents. You already have everything you need to be a success. It's time to trust in yourself and let go of the fear that's kept you from moving forward.

I want to leave you with a question. Because questions are my thing.

What is the worst that would happen if you went all in on your dream? No excuses, no second guessing. No asking for permission. Just running with it?

What's really stopping you from making all your dreams a reality?

About the Author

Through her signature programs, personal branding expert and business mentor Alisha Whaley helps women and mompreneurs transform their business and lifestyle into one they have always dreamed of. Her passion is teaching you how to dream bigger, find the courage to take imperfect action and RISE to new levels of success, over and over again.

As a wife, mom to twin boys, and the CEO of ALICOLE, Alisha knows the life of a busy entrepreneur all too well. With over a decade of graphic design experience, Alisha has created a proven method for Simplifying, Strengthening, and Scaling a business with a personalized brand strategy. She is the host of *The Next Level You* podcast, the creator of the Champagne Branding Method, as well as the founder of the DREAM.COURAGE.RISE. Academy.

Alisha is on a mission to help as many women as she can take the guesswork out of branding to create the lifestyle and brand of their dreams.

Website: www.alicole.co
Facebook: / alicole.co
Email: info@alicoleco.com

Anja Ekstrøm

I never would have imagined it possible but right now, I'm at the top of my game.

I'm shooting commercial campaigns for big brands, getting published in international magazines and appearing on national TV. I am giving lectures and private tuition in photography for people worldwide and shooting campaigns all over the world. Put simply: I'm living the dream I never thought I'd be able to.

Thinking about where I've come from, the knowledge of my life now sometimes takes my breath away because I am just so damn proud. Comparing where I was eight years ago with where I am now makes for two **VERY** different scenarios and had you asked past-me to imagine my present life, I would have laughed on the outside and cried with jealousy on the inside. I know - some people will take my pride and think, "who does she think she is?" After all, that's not the "Danish way" as we are raised with a little thing called *jantelov*, which basically means that you are no better than the person next to you. In my home country, it's not well thought of to be vocal about your accomplishments, but...I don't care. This is a big deal for me.

Let's take it back to the start of my journey.

Eight years ago, I was looking back on a 15- year office career. I had never had a creative thought before yet I caught myself thinking (several times): *is this really what I get? Is this truly my life?* I felt somewhat invisible. I changed jobs every two to four years but that was my "normal" so I didn't think more of it. That was just the way it was. As a person, I have always been very outgoing and, thanks to my office jobs in service functions, I learned to talk to anyone, no matter their age, status or background. I would "meet" you where you were and the conversation would run smoothly. I was the sweet and funny girl in the group, with a sense of humor that would embarrass a truck driver - I guess the term, "read the room" would apply pretty perfectly here, actually - but, over time, my work began to feel like "going through the motions." The weekends felt sacred but they always ended with the same small ache in my stomach on Sunday evenings, knowing a new (LONG) workweek would start the

next day. I had this feeling more times that I can count.....
looking back, I wish I could tell myself: *don't worry Anja, your*
life is soon going to be an adventure!

Nowadays, my life is filled with pride and fulfilment of what
I have built and achieved in eight short years. For me the
weekend now comes as a surprise as I never feel the need to
look at the time when I work.

The Calling

ONE DAY a friend of mine asked me: *"could you take a portrait*
of me? I am doing an art exhibition and need a portrait for the press
release". My first response was a resounding 'NO' as I had no
experience of any kind of photography and I wanted no part
in that. When pushed a little more, I told him that if I could
make every decision on location, styling and vibe I would do
it.

That was when the spark was lit. I knew it right then and
there. Even though I had no technical skill and no experience,
I knew I wanted to do this again – and soon.

Knowing that my small house camera wouldn't cut it, I
upgraded to a used semi-professional camera, bought every

gadget I could think of and, just like that, I decided I was ready!! After that I Just let it RIP!

I was invited by another and professional photographer to tag along on his upcoming photoshoot to just observe how he interacted and composed the picture; how he worked in general. He told me to bring my new camera and that I was welcome to do a little "shooting" of my own on the side, as long as it wasn't disturbing for him or the client. I was beyond excited but very, very nervous. What I hadn't realised was that my experience with VIP clients in my previous jobs had given me the skills I needed to keep on a straight (poker) face, which I did throughout.

This particular day was a big one. On the location I unpacked the new(ish) camera I had bought. With absolutely no idea about anything, I switched "automatic" off and changed it to "manual". I had no previous learning about what all the buttons did but gave each one a try. I tried turning a knob and CLICK... *"Oh, okay,"*... Pressing a button... CLICK... *"Aaah yes! So that influences that!"* and so on. I learnt through trial and error.. It was scary to know absolutely nothing about photography but, at the same time, I remember it as a very exciting time. The time I discovered myself.

The photographer I was with saw my photos and said: *"they are actually pretty decent! Let's include them in the pile for the client to choose from."* He only did that once, as the client chose five out of eight that were mine. I learned a lot that day: not just about the camera, either. Because that was the day I found my calling.

Trial and Error

Over the next months I practiced a lot. I shot everything from lifestyle and cars to people, fashion and beauty. I even tried weddings and baby-shoots, keen to find my way.

I quickly learned that I really loved the creative side. In the fashion and beauty universe there were no limits to what I could create. The colours, texture, expression, vibes,.... I loved it all and knew this had to be my path. I still had a full-time office job at this point but, for the very first time in my life, I felt CONNECTED! I had found my passion.

At first, I was a little bit angry that I found my passion so late in life – I was 37!! Why did I have to go through so many years without a fire in me?! - but then I turned it around. Really, I was lucky to have found my passion at all as some people never do. They go through life never knowing that feeling of contentment.

For a while, I kept my photography as a hobby. I have always charged money for my work but started out softly. As I already had plenty of adult responsibilities such as a mortgage and bills, I still kept my office job for the great steady paycheck but kept dreaming about that day where I could quit my day job and do it full time. As I was 37 with a loan in the bank, a car and an apartment, I didn't think this would be realistic for me, until the day that changed everything.

A Leap of Faith

I got to a point where I had the chance to get a studio. Me and three others took the lease. I was the "boss" and they rented a spot in the studio from me, so we divided it into 4 equal parts.

Now, I had a playground of my own and at this point had also realized the importance of a new genre in my business - portraits - and a studio was, without a doubt, needed for that.

I was still having the "Sunday stomachache" in regards to my office job which was very stressful and demanding, so I looked at my boyfriend (now husband) and said: *"What if I took one day a week away from the office and invested it into my photography?"* We did the math and decided we could still afford food, so it was a-GO!

This was a very big step for me. I was missing four days from my salary every month and I also had to make sure the lease on the studio was paid. The pressure was on: my photography side-hustle had to earn money.

Despite the risks, it was the best decision I ever made. I quickly learned that the more time I invested into my business, the more clients would come my way. It felt as if the universe knew what I wanted and had answered me.

Of course, the more my fire burned for photography, the less interested I became in my office job. For me, a workweek had to move by quickly so I could get back to my studio. My 30-minute lunch breaks became anti-social as I needed to reply to emails, answer makeup artists and models on Facebook as well as decide things for future shoots. I needed to make sure everything was set up so when my time at the studio came, I could hit the ground running.

It became a full time job without me knowing it, on top of the full time office job I was actually doing. If I wasn't in the studio, I was planning, editing, retouching or networking. It didn't take long for me to realise that something had to give.

I was still new in the game here – feeling my way through. I was teaching myself everything - not only about the camera technology but also about lighting, photoshop and exporting files as well as how to interact with clients, models and brands. I learned early on that I couldn't read a manual - I needed everything to be shown to me. That's when I realised I had to find someone to teach me in person.

I entered the Facebook groups, and asked all my rookie questions about this and that and... I found a WALL of silence peppered with just a few grumpy replies with a collective meaning: *"Find it on Youtube."*

This was very disappointing to me. How and why would this be the response? I quickly figured it was a mixture of nerves at helping a competitor in the making and also that they were tired of answering the same questions over and over again to people that they considered amateurs.

As a new photographer, that was very demotivating but, at the same time, I felt the fire in me to prove them wrong. In spite of my lack of technical skills I *knew* I had something and I would stop at nothing to show them!

Fortunately, not ALL of the group members were hostile and I met a select few that helped me a lot. In this period, I grew and evolved so quickly and I will be forever grateful to those people who helped shape me into what I am today. I am now proud to call them my friends and industry peers.

Early on, even back when I started, I learned that the social media platforms would be vital for my business. I had the perfect visual platforms right at my fingertips and so I built a presence across Facebook, Instagram and LinkedIn. I learned a lot here. You have to be consistent and find your own way of representing your work and personality as these platforms are there to represent you and not vice versa. It was important that my followers on each platform felt my personal presence rather than just seeing a gallery.

The Next Level

At this time I was truly growing as a business. I had a celebrity portfolio, solid brands on my reference list but then one day in 2016 I had another major breakthrough - one that would turn out to be career-making.

I got an email from a little-known brand called L'Oreal (I still remember the screams of joy on the inside) who had followed me on Instagram for a while and were in love with my work. They loved the "honesty" in my work and wanted to hire me for a roundtrip in the Nordic countries. Whaaat?! I was still fairly new to the game and yet there I was, negotiating with L'Oreal! If that's not crazy, I don't know what is.

I ran to my boss at the office job and immediately handed in my resignation. I knew that I would earn two to three months' salary on the L'Oreal job so if I was ever going to jump, it had to be now. I almost caved with the anxiety of not having a salary every month but despite the nerves, I have never felt so much peace inside. This was what I was meant to do. This was my dream. And it was time to move.

I hit the ground flying after that. I had a full schedule for a long time and still do to this day, but (yes, there is a but!) I suffer from "imposter syndrome." One day I can be on Cloud Nine and the next, I feel like an imposter incapable of anything and wondering when "they" will find out I am without talent. The down days are, thankfully, not that often but still something I battle with once in a while. When I am low, I just take a look back to see what I have already accomplished and my mood lifts immediately: I am a POWERWOMAN.

How To Achieve Rapid Success

Shortly after going solo, I learned about SEO (Search Engine Optimization) and what it can do for a business. Within a month of implementing these steps, I was getting four times the amount of customer inquiries I had been before. Today, I am at the top of google searches and proud to be.

Here's what you need to know.

1. Get your Seo game ON.

Google placements do make a BIG difference and, yes, spend the money on a professional SEO expert - it's worth the investment.

2. ALWAYS maintain your social media as you never know who is watching you.

This I know for a fact, as I landed both L'Oreal and several other clients through here. Consistency is key.

3. Don't try to get everything perfect before starting. Adjust and make it better as you go, otherwise you will never start. There will always be something to do better or differently but remember: you attract what you send out, so if you stop before beginning, that's the energy the world will see and deem "not credible". Just believe in what you have and OWN it as is, and the rest of the world will follow.

4. NEVER underestimate the power of networking.

Networking is truly the key. I learned that my network is just as important as the photography itself. I have seen better photographers than me not make it because they either don't want to network or don't understand the power of it. I still get recommended for jobs by people I have never met in person because they connected with me online and therefore see my name, work and face on a regular basis. I am often at the forefront of their mind so pop up if someone needs a photographer.

5. AIM BIG. Never settle.

Always strive towards your goal, big or small. I always aim for things that seem a little out of reach and usually end up getting the job by doing so because we are all way more capable than we give ourselves credit for. I promise you it's worth the learning and challenges along the way.

6. It's never just about your talent/product.

If you don't take the steps above, you will find it can be an uphill climb. If you follow the steps above, you have made the path much easier for yourself to succeed.

I am the one one in my family who runs their own business, so I had no one to learn from. I learned it all by myself and by asking or studying other business owners. I found out that our "gut feeling" is a magnificent tool and I use mine often in my decision-making and, more times than I can count, my gut has been right!

Today, I feel like a totally different person in another universe compared to how I used to feel just a few years ago. I love my life now. Finding this kind of career bliss takes dedication and hard work but you have to ask yourself, what does it matter if you love what you do?

I get to travel with my work and experience the world, I am published in more magazines than I can count and, I would say, I have succeeded in creating a brand many know and use.

If I could leave you with one lesson I wish I'd learnt earlier myself, it would be to believe in yourself and, if your financials allow it, take the plunge and go all in. There is nothing more satisfying than being your own boss. Make sure you pay any kindness you receive forward and don't become one of those nay-sayers many meet early on in their careers.

Lastly, I'll leave you with a quote: *"Talent is nothing without courage,"* and I think that's true. It takes a lot of courage to do something this big for yourself but, as the title says, I did it and so can you! The rewards are never-ending on so many levels and you'll never regret investing in yourself.

About the Author

Anja is a self taught passionate photographer, who automatically connects with the people in front of her camera. This ability - alongside her amazing creative mind - creates unbelievable results, whether it's portrait, international fashion or a beauty campaign she's working on. With the ability to make those around her feel at ease, her understanding and passion for creative storytelling, each piece she presents is a work of art.

When you meet Anja, there is no doubt in your mind that she loves what she does. Anja is a hands-on photographer who she loves being a part of the whole process from start to finish. Through her detail-orientated approach to everything from the planning to finding the right models, makeup looks, styling the wardrobe and the retouch, Anja always gets a perfect result.

Website: www.anjaekstroem.dk

Facebook: www.facebook.com / aekstroem

Instagram: www.instagram.com / anjaekstroem

Email: anja@anjaekstroem.dk

Picture credit: Gary Britton

Evelyne Brink

"I don't think he's going to make it."

This is not what any new parent wants to hear.

It's the 13th January 2012. We are sitting in the quiet room at St. Thomas' Hospital in London and the surgeon is barely looking up from the floor.

"He lost all his small intestine. We've never seen anything like it."

He's a seasoned medic and the weight of his words leaves little room to breathe.

How would you feel if you were told your new-born baby wasn't going to live?

This was meant to be the happiest day of my life.

My dream of becoming a mother included lattes with the

ladies and glowing with pride pushing a cool pram. It was about feeling more love than ever and feeling empowered to discover the world with this new little person, yet here I was, sitting with my tender perineal stitches bleeding through thick pads on a hard NHS chair, just aching to hold my baby. But my baby is wrapped in countless wires and I am dependent on hospital staff to hand him to me when the doctors aren't with him or when he isn't resting. I only get to hold him for a few minutes every few hours, making the most of the little time we were told we'll have together.

Surgeries, cannulas, dressing changes, emptying of bags, tubes, wires, scans, monitors. The best-case scenario: two-four years in hospital and a life on machines. The worst? A few days.

How on earth were we supposed to live our full potential now? And did that even matter?

Another Lifetime

At a conference, five years earlier, I had a calling. One speaker after another talked about how they'd gone from rags to riches. Although it was inspiring, it was rather money- focussed; a masculine go-getter-wow-show. The storyline always spanned from failure to success; poor to rich.

I sat there thinking, *"Where is the woman talking about life as it really is? Beyond all this 'business success equals happiness' stuff? Real life. Inner worlds. Impact also beyond personal wealth. Finding our true power."*

And, just then, my body started to tingle and I felt this presence saying, *"She's sitting in your seat."*

My body shivered. I had just settled into a "normal" life. With a real job. And a salary. After over a decade of fending for myself, often struggling to make ends meet as a performing artist, I had finally made it into the corporate world and I was doing well. I was loving the safety of employment and I had no intention of jumping back into uncertainty.

And yet that voice was a calling from the deep and I knew it wasn't going away. I had to listen.

So I told my boss about my vision and quit my cushy job.

Two weeks later, the BBC auditioned for the nation's best

tribute acts. I heard the call. I answered. And lo and behold, that is how I became the UK's number one Madonna impersonator. I was living the dream. My plan of gaining fame and being able to influence from the top seemed to be coming together at last! Confidence and transformational coaching would simply be a natural follow-up act from this.

It was 2008 and I was on BBC1 with Graham Norton with millions of viewers glued to their TV screens, watching this live show. I was ready to perform "Material Girl" as Madonna. This was my big moment, after over 13 years as a performer.

It was going to be amazing.

Imagine you're with me on that bench in the glamorous TV studio at the BBC. Me in the pink cocktail dress and a blonde wig, with diamante jewellery dripping off me and my pink satin gloves. The excitement is palpable. My amazing hot dancers are in the green room.

But the thing is, I really don't want to be on TV tonight. I want to be with my family, in a different country altogether. Because I had been told that very morning that my beloved grandfather had died and I was going to miss the funeral because I was too busy becoming famous, imitating someone I was not.

After the show, there was none of the fame I'd been prepping for. The telephone was silent.

My life felt so empty. *I* was empty. I felt I had nothing left to give. Everything felt meaningless. I didn't know where to go from here.

My 85-year-old great-aunt shook me up. She was a trained psychotherapist with a strong Hungarian accent and a sharp tongue.

"You are not crying about your grandfather. You are crying about yourself!"

And she was right.

I didn't know who to be. How to be. What to do next. Where to gain my motivation from. I remember part of me wanted to push ahead and carve out a career in coaching and performing but I had no energy to support it.

How many of us keep functioning, soldiering on with barely

any "gas in the tank"?

Then I heard my inner voice suggesting that I should simply follow inspiration for a month. So I did. Which meant mostly doing nothing and only getting up for things that actually excited me. And interestingly enough, despite mostly sitting in a chair being quite bored, I landed back on my feet: gigs came in, energy returned, tours were booked, and the opportunity arose to co-write a show and co-star at the Edinburgh Festival.

Next, I created my own show and raised the £25,000 needed to produce it - all in the same year the financial crisis hit. I still smile when I tell this story. How did that happen? It certainly wasn't "grit and determination." I was guided by inspiration and I was powered by pleasure because, as I'd learnt, true self-expression is very pleasurable.

After a successful run at the prestigious Edinburgh Festival which I very much enjoyed, I decided that rather than milking the show on national tours, boring myself with the repetition of the material, I could keep following the path of my true desire, so I focused on building my coaching business. I grossed $50k in my first year. This was my ideal transition to starting family life.

Early Days

Six weeks after my son was born, he was still with us, alive, fighting.

I was tied to the hospital, stuck on a square meter of space, day by day. There was nowhere to go and nothing to do.

Despite this, I soon found myself thriving. It surprised me, too. I thought that you are meant to be as down as your circumstances, but it turns out nobody can decide that but you. And as down as I was after the glamorous TV experience, in this seemingly dire scenario, my spirit was on fire and I was THERE.

I dressed well; I put on make-up. I spent much of my day topless for skin-to-skin contact with my baby. I loved all that skin contact and the warm temperature of the unit. Everyone saw my breasts. I had no time for embarrassment and shame. I did what was right and I felt so free.

I started going swimming twice a week. That felt "crazy". It meant leaving my baby alone that bit more to replenish myself. Swimming feels luxurious and clearing to me. At the time, many of my thoughts whirled around guilt and self-approval. *How can you go to the pool while your baby is in intensive care?* I made it my meditation to breathe out all the judgements of how selfish I felt and, as a result, I was rewarded with increased energy and sanity.

6 months in, I took up ballroom dancing - a stark contrast to the medical day to day - and again it fuelled me with the glamour and pleasure which built my capacity to deal with the rest.

The Burnout

Eight months in, I had learned all my son's complex care procedures and, to my delight, the doctors agreed that I could take over and take him home. That meant I was replacing two doctors and a full-time nurse, twenty-four hours a day. It meant being responsible for giving infusions into the central blood stream via a vein above his heart each night. It meant getting up several times each night. It meant recognising emergencies in time to get back to the hospital.

I had been my own woman since I had left school. As an international entertainer, recording artist, entrepreneur, comedienne, impersonator, author, coach and speaker, I had lived in New York, Berlin and London. I had travelled the world. I had followed my dreams.

But now I was trading all this in to have my child.

The doctors said I'd never work again because the care of my son would be too much. I experienced in my body what they meant. I was used to doing a lot. I normally had buckets of energy but now I found myself becoming so tired I even dreamt at night of collapse. I died in my dreams several times. They said that it is not uncommon for parents in my situation to contemplate suicide. And a few years in even I, who was known to be mentally buoyant, understood why.

When you give up your personal life, desires and all that you "are" to care for another person, there is a hefty price to pay.

The consequences range from adrenal fatigue and burnout, to depression and illness. Then there is the numbness. Losing a sense of who you are. Settling for less, more and more often. Slowly dying inside.

A life without pleasure loses the juice. In this bleak time, I came to see pleasure as a luxury you have to be able to afford and, at that time, it was too expensive for me.

Another Shock

I have made a few of my biggest dreams a reality.

I certainly wanted my dream of becoming a mum to come true, but I hadn't expected this heavy reality of what giving birth to a new human could mean. It turns out there are no guarantees your child is healthy, easy to deal with, or that it's going to be anywhere near how you imagined it. We have to face that and find the grace within the situation.

And, in the darkness of this desperate situation, I indeed found a secret that liberated me.

The doctors had predicted that working and caring for my son would be impossible. Two years in, I was coaching, ran workshops at the BBC and Channel 4. I wrote my book *It Takes Guts: A Story of Love, Hope and a Missing Bowel*.

How did I do that?

The secret lay in following my desire and fuelling myself with pleasure, as I had done so many times before. It seems counterintuitive when you are in survival mode but it is indeed the golden key to creating what you really want.

But following desire does not exempt you from the mundane layers of reality. Real life was certainly happening: real loneliness, real fatigue, real relationship struggles, real lack of time. Real mundane stuff and then some.

You can probably imagine that I was scared of having a second child.

When my daughter was born I was overjoyed. She was so beautiful and I even experienced an orgasmic birth.

All was well for 3 days.

After that, she stopped feeding well and started making strange noises. Reluctantly, I went to the hospital to get her checked.

Oxygen measurement went on. Baby was snatched out of my arms. Alarms were going off.

As it turned out, she had heart failure due to 4 heart defects.

We were hospitalised and within hours she looked very much like her brother back in the early days: nasal tubes, wires and cannulas. But this time they didn't say, *"We don't know."* They said, *"We can handle this."* This was an upgraded medical experience, version 2.0.

Open heart surgery was the prognosis.

We spent a month in the hospital. My friends would bring my son to me so that I could see him and do his weekly dressing change. At one point, he had a blood infection and ended up an inpatient too.

How did I survive that?

You probably guessed it by now: I recharged with pleasure. This time, it was reading English Literature, something I had never before "had time for" and thoroughly enjoyed.

A month later we were released and able to go back home and, miraculously, we were on medicine and observation rather than surgery. I had now witnessed two medical miracles first-hand. However, the daily care routine was gruesome again. I had to mix and administer medicines ten times a day, feed her through a tube in her nose every three hours and express my milk in between. Twenty-four seven.

"This is too much," I said. *"Superwoman is giving up!"*

I made the decision to surrender to each moment (or whatever you call it when you can't take more than one step at a time).

My daughter recovered without surgery.

I survived giving those treatments and she came off them gracefully a few months later.

By now, my son was thriving and living wirelessly in the day, even attending mainstream school.

In the name of respect

I'd love to say that all was well and I was now living my dream life.

But life at home wasn't fun.

A colleague suggested that I was a victim of emotional abuse, an observation I did not appreciate at all. I am a life coach and I consider myself to be a strong woman, not a victim. But the way things were between my partner and me, it would have been kinder to separate respectfully than continue as we were.

45

Something in me was so afraid to step up. I questioned myself constantly, which left me doubting my mental stability, sanity, health. I felt so dependent, like I couldn't cope with everything on my own. As a child of divorced parents, the last thing I wanted was a failed marriage and the devastation it leaves all-round.

Even the lawyer confirmed that separating was impossible, financially. Logistically, we already knew it was chaos, and medically... well. Don't even go there.

One evening, after a series of events that forced me to accept the reality of the situation, I had a strong calling. The voice was clear: "In the name of self-love and respect, please go. Go now."

So, impossible or not, I left. I stayed at different friends' houses during their holidays and had the kids four days a week.

I found my new home within a few months and it was what I had asked for:

"A view on the green with birdsong; quiet and friendly. Good energy, light, spacious, in budget, close to the station and in the

same borough (due to the care package and medications needed) and if there could be an American type fridge that makes ice cubes that my son so likes, that would be great!"

Sounds utopian? I know. But I got exactly that.

However, I had lost my relationship of almost 13 years, the family structure and support of his family, my foundation, the house and most of what was in it. I lost my financial security, my sense of belonging, the garden with the hammock and the newly refurbished outhouse office conversion I had invested my last business savings into.

I also lost my tolerance for unacceptable behaviour towards me.

Rock Bottom

I'd love to say that moving out, following my intuition and recommitting to my own path, was the way to immediate success. But before I could come up, I went down. Really down. Thankfully, I signed my first coaching apprentice and another yearlong client.

Other than that, I found myself pretty unable to work. My

concentration wouldn't hold very long. I could attach to my passion and sense of self for a day and lose it for weeks. Months. Everything was too much. Getting dressed was often a challenge. I was able to function for all my kids' medical care and basic needs. Other than that, I had no more capacity.

I experienced mental cloudiness, confusion, anguish, anxiety, extreme fatigue, sadness, anger, rage, tension, sleeplessness, memory loss, apathy, loss of appetite, lack of energy and low moods.

I was in deep pain.

If you had asked me, "What do you do?" I wouldn't have known how to answer. Often, I had no grip on a sense of self; it was all changing or dissolving into a soup of nothing.

But that's what needed to happen.

If you cut a caterpillar cocoon open you will find neither a caterpillar nor a butterfly in it. You will find soup. DNA soup. That's where my personality and life went. Into the soup of potential. It felt pretty yucky.

There was only one strand of energy that came back to nurture me and fanned the flames again… And so I followed that:

The path of pleasure.

In this phase, I discovered the potency of sex. It was a surprising change for me because, after years of keeping my head down, surviving the medical madness and then the relationship dynamics that left me feeling broken and unwanted, to think about wild, passionate sex was a far cry from my reality.

I really thought no one would want me now that my body had been spoiled by childbirth and nursing. Oh, how wrong I was, and how good it is to be wrong sometimes.

I discovered the bliss which the journey of feminine pleasure allows. I discovered that the womanly arts are based on allowing yourself to receive and surrender to the experience fully. To dare to speak up and express your desire in the moment. To learn to appreciate every sensation.

I dared to allow myself to feel more. I expanded my ability to receive, to have, to hold, to enjoy. I grew the sense of deserving without the entitlement to it.

How good can you have it? Will you allow more pleasure, more bliss?

Climax is a way for the body to show its threshold, but what happens when you relax into the intensity rather than chase the end destination? These became generative explorations and my energy and capacity started rising.

My patience for my children came back, I grew in capacity. My ability to concentrate and hold my attention returned. I've been able to graciously implement some healthy routines to give our life structure, reducing some of the chaos. Admin gets done without drama. I'm more often living in an inspired state.

The high energy Evelyne returned to shine her light on stages, videos and the playground.

I've regained the ability to organise myself and my business. My decision-making power recovered. When I'm on the phone with authorities, I can often make them laugh at the madness. That to me is a sure-fire sign that I'm on. I've enjoyed writing and performing stand-up comedy.

My next step is to take the business up where it belongs!

Video Impact - Be Your Best Self On Camera found its feet just as the pandemic hit.

I had been working with successful business owners on harnessing the power of expression on video before and 2020 was the right time to expand the program.

As Covid19 started to hit the world, my energy was ready to step up my leadership in the world. I had been crisis trained for eight years, I was solid and ready to help and transmit new possibilities. I grew my business to six figures in three short months. But that was just the tip of the iceberg. My real business gem is *Business by Pleasure* - a revolutionary feminine business approach. I coach high-achieving business women in how to power their business and life through extreme well-being. Pleasure in every sense of the word to create the seemingly impossible for themselves.

Powered by Pleasure

I want to see a world where living with and from pleasure is the obvious path. Where we love ourselves and others more and have capacity for the joy life has to offer on a daily basis. I stand for wild creativity, for making the impossible happen even if you think you can't or shouldn't or simply pee your pants.

1. Acknowledge your struggles.

It brings tears to my eyes to see how women struggle, often because of not understanding how their world actually works, having been indoctrinated into a very male-dominated way of operating.

2. When in doubt, always turn back to pleasure.

When we learn to use pleasure as a guiding path, it makes miracles happen. It's time to let go of the shackles of the "good woman," become unashamedly visible and let your voice be heard. And when I say *voice*, I mean the uniqueness of your personality and the wisdom from your womb.

We can be unstoppably gentle and also put our foot down. But without our feminine energy and presence, we have nothing. With our pleasure power, we can have everything.

About the Author

Evelyne Brink is an author, mother, coach and speaker with a prolific background in entertainment - particularly one-woman shows, comedy, singing-songwriting and acting.

With 5 published CDs, a signing to Sony music and three previous books, she travelled the world as Europes' No.1 Madonna Impersonator as seen on TV.

Having been coaching professionally for almost 20 years, Evelyne founded the Business by Pleasure Club to elevate high-achieving women into living a life and business that is nourishing and enjoyable and which also makes the world a better place. She has built a six-figure business with kids at home whilst working part time. To keep happy during the pandemic, she enjoys watching movies with her kids whilst huddled up in her sauna blanket.

Website: www.brinkcoaching.com

Facebook: www.facebook.com/evelyne.brink/
www.facebook.com/BRINKCOACHING123/

Instagram: www.instagram.com/evelynebrink/
@evelynebrink

Email: hello@brinkcoaching.com

Heather Russo

I don't have a get-rich-quick story but what I do have is a story that will unfold and show you that, if I can build wealth, so can you. I hope that no matter where you are in your financial journey, you will know it is not too late; that it matters more what you do with your money than the amount you make and there is no debt too big to overcome. That you have the power to change your financial future.

It has been a journey for me to get to this day. Despite all the difficulties 2020 brought, it has catapulted me into a new club: I am officially a multi-millionaires club member - something that feels so surreal that, sometimes, I have to pinch myself.

This was not always the case. Five years ago, I was over $217,000 in debt and now, just a few short years later, I have a net worth of over $3.5m. Those days, just a few years ago, seemed so overwhelming and hopeless. I had been studying personal finance for 30 years and had done well managing my money yet could not get ahead. With massive student loan debt, it seemed impossible to be debt-free. I will admit I had some dark days back then, but no matter what, I never gave up trying - something my husband would attribute to my dogged determination. I have overwhelming gratitude for where I am today, but am also not surprised - I always knew, deep down, that one day I would be wealthy and was made for a significant purpose; it was an intention I held from my youth.

Growing up, I was not blessed with a silver spoon in my mouth. It was more like a plastic spork. We struggled for food and never had financial stability, even though my mom earned a decent living and had a stable job. All I knew was that I did not want my life to be like that when I grew up. So I set out to read every book and attend every seminar I could on personal finance at the ripe old age of 18. I am grateful for that childhood; it kept me focused and inspired to be and do better and now, in my late 40s, I have done it. As I said, it's certainly not a get-rich-quick story!

Now, here I am celebrating my success and having the opportunity to run a company that educates others on their journeys to a wealthy life. All my life, it seems, has brought me to this moment: running a business that gives the opportunity of financial freedom to thousands of people. It never gets old - the letters and emails I get from clients, how their lives have changed, and how many, for the first time, have hope for their financial futures. My business continues to flourish, creating multiple income streams each month, just by word of mouth. I have finally arrived.

Where my passion for business started

My journey to success as a money coach was not my first career, although it is truly my passion and purpose, so is most likely to be my last.

Having got married at 18 to my high school sweetheart and had a baby a year later, my first passion was my family. I mostly held basic office jobs and was content to work and take care of them. When things didn't turn out to be *"happily ever after"*, I realized I needed to take care of myself financially. Still, in a worker's mindset, I got a job in middle management to have better pay and benefits to care for my kids and me. I was 29 before I really started asking myself what I wanted to do when I grew up. Before then, I just took what life offered me.

Growing up, I had had terrible acne and struggled with it until my 20s. I realized I wanted to learn how to heal my skin and help others do the same, so I went off to school to be an Esthetician. Being an *"all in"* kind of person, I quit my job, put the tuition on a 12-month interest-free credit card, lived off my savings very frugally and went to school full time to get my 600 hours completed and take my state licensing test as fast as possible.

I started my first job as an esthetician at a spa and loved it. It was the first time I felt like I had a career and I was excited to go to work every day. That was a first. It did not take long for me to realize I wanted to work for myself so, a year later, I took the leap and opened my own business in a rented room in a salon. I had never imagined myself as an entrepreneur before this; I had always said I was not a career woman, just happy to work a basic job and take care of my family. Boy, was I wrong! Despite having to work three other jobs while I got my business going, I'd had my first taste and was hooked. Fast forward a few years and I'd branched out even more by opening my own wellness spa.

In order to offer my clients more, I continued my education. I became a licensed massage therapist, certified yoga therapist and nutritionist. I did that for over five years but the strain of keeping so many balls in the air left me exhausted. That's when I developed an autoimmune illness. By this time I had remarried and my new husband was offered his dream job, so I had the opportunity to sell my business and, for the first time since I was 15, to be unemployed. It was unnerving, to say the least, but it gave me some space and time to think what was my next venture. Still enjoying esthetics but realizing I could not go back into the treatment room with the way my health was, I decided to do my work online and launched the first online virtual Esthetics services.

Though I did this for a few years, it just didn't fulfill me the way I'd hoped so, in 2019, I stopped that business. Once again I had space and time to re-evaluate my career path. I hired a career coach and discovered what I had always known: I love personal finance.

Throughout my life I had studied and applied what I had learnt about my own finances and helped friends and family with theirs, it had just never occurred to me that I could do it as a career. I have a significant passion for assisting people in getting their money working for them and creating financial stability, so I leapt again into a career field that I had no prior professional experience in.

Let me tell you - it felt much more comfortable mentally doing this in my late twenties than late forties. I had been well-versed in brick and mortar business practices in my last career but this time I was required to build a whole new type of business online and from scratch. Despite the challenges, I knew in my heart that this was the right path; that this is my purpose and that I had the chance to change lives. After all, I'd done it for myself as well as countless friends and family. So in late 2019, *Your Money Success Coach* was born.

Major challenges

So here I was, so excited that I had finally found my one true passion and that I was going all-in to bring my services to the public. I honestly felt like I would have tons of people reaching out to me right away; I mean, who would not want to learn how to make the most out of the money they are making and get it working for them while becoming debt-free in the process? When that didn't happen, I was feeling entirely defeated and wondered if I was on the right path. This taught me an important lesson: just because I love to learn about money and how to use it efficiently and effectively, doesn't mean that everyone else does.

Money comes with some big emotions attached to it for

better or worse. Many do not want to talk about it or even deal with it as it will have them dealing with themselves and their choices in the process. I also had to deal with objections such as, *"aren't you just an esthetician? What makes you think you can teach me about money?"* I had my own money hang-ups - in my family, you did not discuss money - so I had never shared my financial journey and accomplishments, so it was no surprise that no one knew of my wisdom and success with money.

The next obstacle was how to reach more people, which I knew had to be done right. I needed an expert, so I hired a business building coach. Early on in my previous businesses, I learned that we could not be experts in everything; we don't have to be. Often, we get paralyzed by the mindset of, *"I have to do it all myself because I have no money to spend."* We take on everything to get the business off the ground thinking it is saving money but the opposite is true - money-making opportunities are lost in the time it takes for you to learn and set something up, not doing things the right way for a specific platform or not appropriately optimizing your business. All of this will cost thousands in lost sales that, if you had just hired an expert for in the first place, you would have had the time to recoup in sales.

If you take nothing else from this section, let it be this: you have permission to get the help you need. Relieve the stress and anxiety of having to do it all, and you will achieve faster and more tremendous success, I promise you!

Even as I started making progress, I still had fears and doubts deep down about whether or not I could be successful in a whole new field. Each set back really did a number on my confidence and mindset. I knew that I could have all the tools but if I couldn't get my head in the game, this business was going nowhere.

The breakthrough

I wish I could tell you there was one incredible magic moment that changed everything but there wasn't; there were 100 little ones over time. I channeled my strengths. My dogged determination did not let me quit when I felt defeated.

Essentially, I kept focusing on my *why*: that I wanted to be a successful money coach so that I could save families from breaking up, as finances are the number one reason for divorce. People get so overwhelmed with debt or large losses of money that they lose hope and give up their lives. Families struggle with money from generation to generation because they don't know how to do better. I knew I had the power to change these outcomes. That *why* and the determination not to give up on these people I had never met but knew I could serve kept me trying day after day. Know your *why,* make it bigger than yourself and you will never give up.

The right people with the right skills came into my life so I hired them for their expertise. I prayed for them daily. I opened myself up to all the possibilities and let the universe deliver them. Sometimes the most magic came when I stopped trying to control and force everything.

I humbled myself and knew when I needed help. When I did that, I found a transformational coach who worked with EFT and overcame my fear and self-doubt, taking my mindset to the next level. Next, an incredible group of women who worked on public speaking together invited me to their group. It helped me overcome my fear of speaking online or on a stage. I got the support to start talking about my financial knowledge and successes and become known as an expert. I used my courage not to be afraid to leap, to try things more significant than I had imagined before.

In those moments, I would often remind myself; I had lost everything before. I had failed and not only survived but eventually thrived.

I have never regretted aiming big as if I didn't win, I always learned. Throughout my life, I have held steadfast to that knowing I had as a teen; that one day, no matter how long it took, I would be wealthy and live a life of purpose. I posted my affirmations to support that belief everywhere. I practiced visualization, visualized my office, my calendar full of clients, and saw their faces. I knew how it all looked, felt, smelled. I knew how I looked and felt, dressed in beautiful clothes, and filled with joy! You are what you think - your thoughts create your reality - so always consider the best of yourself, your business and your success.

What you need to know

1. Never stop learning and growing

Create a daily habit of learning. Whether it's the subject matter that's your specialty, learning public speaking, sales, technology, or mastering your mindset. Knowledge is power. Continuous learning will keep your confidence and motivation up. Know your strengths and your weaknesses and set out to sharpen the skills you need to. We all have something to learn, ALWAYS. It does not have to take much time; I block out just 20 minutes a day to listen to a podcast, read a blog, watch a video or read a chapter in a book. It doesn't matter what medium it is; it just matters that you commit to it and do it daily. I like to pick a subject matter for the week and will dive into all those ways of learning on that topic each day for that week. Make this ritual a part of your day and watch how your business changes.

2. Dress for the success you want

This not only serves to strengthen your brand but it also keeps up your confidence. Especially if your business has you working from home, where it's easy to stay unshowered and in your yoga pants and t-shirt all day. We all have experienced a day where we love how we look - the outfit, hair and make-up on fleek. We feel powerful, confident and high energy. When we do this, we are more productive, creative and willing to take risks. It's not just about the outside trimmings; it's a matter of living your goals and dreams inside and out. When you take that confidence and power you feel from the outside and combine it with the inner confidence and knowledge you have in your purpose, it means that you believe in it absolutely and will pursue it relentlessly. It becomes your way of being, meaning that you dress, talk, and behave consistently with your ultimate aspirations. Bring this energy to your business every day and watch your success soar.

3. Develop a shield of armor

I find this one especially important for all of us. It can wreak havoc on your success if you allow it to penetrate. We all face rejection, ridicule, jealousy and people forming opinions of us that we may disagree with. It just seems to be the human nature of success. If you allow yourself to attach to these things, it will keep you in doubt, anxiety, fear and cause you to shrink down and not become the influential person your subconscious fears. When you are ready to start your day, put on your mental armour of light, the universe, the infinite creator, or whatever it is you like to call it. Mentally and physically see and feel that protection around you. When you encounter one of these events happening, stop and take a breath and then take another one. Instead of attaching to their words, say, *"that is an interesting point of view."* Remember: someone else's opinion does not define you unless YOU let it. Most often, the other person is simply projecting their personal pain onto you. The sooner you can connect to the fact that what they are saying has nothing to do with you or your actions, the faster you can move on from it.

4. Remember you are not alone

Success is not meant for just some of us - it is in all of us! You can have the business of your dreams. If you already have it, celebrate it - OFTEN. If you are struggling, you are not alone; we all have highs and lows. No matter where you are in your business, know that I have been there too. Don't suffer alone - reach out for support from business professionals, friends, or family to help you achieve your dreams. The one thing I did that added to my success the most besides hiring the right professionals was to form a circle of other influential, life-changing entrepreneurs. I knew they would know what I was feeling; I could lean on them when I was stuck, in a rut, or at the end of my rope. They listened, cheered me on, and offered support and solutions. Find your people, people like you who share the passion of entrepreneurship that you can support and support you. Success is sweeter when shared.

About the Author

Heather has studied personal finance for over 30 years and specialized in wealth strategies for the last 10 years. She has mentored and learned from some of the top wealth creators around the world. She has also made practically every mistake you can make with money and it has cost her dearly. But she never gave up and, after digging herself out of almost $217k of debt, she realized how much easier life can be when you get your money working for instead of against you. Once she had put the systems and strategies of the wealthy she had learned into place, she went from deep into debt to a multi- millionaire in five years. Heather has made it her life's mission to help families, couples and individuals create a life of financial security, no matter their income.

Website: www.yourmoneysuccesscoach.com
Facebook: www.facebook.com/yourmoneysuccesscoach
Email: heather@yourmoneysuccesscoach

Jessica Hughes

Where it all started

Hot coffee in hand, I walk the twenty feet from my back door to my art studio. Snow clings tightly to every branch. Another winter wonderland. And another day clean and sober. It's day 1,076 of my new life.

I face the massive canvas in my brightly-lit studio, loosely holding a brush loaded with pale pink, drips sprinkling the floor as I pause, ready to make that first touch with canvas. I let the bristles drag, slow at first, then end in a wild scribble. Color peeks through the thick layers of textured paint. The layers of my story peek through. Some dark, some quiet, many vibrant. The nuance of emotion captured concretely, reflected back.

The music is loud and wild. Just like me. The REAL me. The once-meek little turtle is finally dancing. Freely. Uninhibited.

No more hiding. No more playing small.

I load the palette knife with a muted turquoise allowing my hand to follow its lead.

This is my 90th painting in four months. I can't even remember what it feels like to be blocked. I paint with abandon - my insides turned outside for all the world to see. I revel in these moments. I am called to do this work, here to serve others as an entrepreneur, teacher, speaker, author and healer.

My foundation in business and life is simply to feel grateful to wake up each day. Three years ago, I had the choice to live or die and I chose life. Everything beyond that is just icing on the cake.

And wow, the icing! It's come so rapidly in just months. $12,000 from the last few weeks of painting sales is sitting in my account. Art collectors and fans from all over the world are buying my paintings as soon as I finish them. My calendar is jammed. I am booked for nine media interviews in the next two weeks. I have a Ted X speech to prepare, courses in therapeutic art to create, and coaching calls in demand. Cameras are staged in all areas of my studio to capture the artist at work on TV. I've just hired help, only months after committing to this dream.

I have been told that I shine now. It is true.

But it wasn't always so easy.

Decades of hiding the shame of my addictions, the eating disorder and unaddressed PTSD are behind me now. The carefully constructed house of cards that was once my life collapsed. I've built a new foundation firmly based on my truth. I love the person I am today. She is radiant, filled with love and fulfilled by purpose.

I am here to speak up - to be an example of hope for anyone in the face of addiction, eating disorders, mental health, and the stigma that surrounds them. I have lived it all. Luckily, I had a strong beginning.

Where it all started

My artist's dream was born in the third grade when my drawing was chosen as the class favorite. I can still remember that rush of pride. I was a shy, whimsical child. Uncomfortable in my own skin, always one step out of place with the norm. But when I realized I could draw, it became my superpower.

In high school I dove deep into my art. The school hosted my one woman show as a senior. I found my calling. I enrolled at Skidmore college as a double art/music major.

Two weeks prior to starting, my still winsome spirit was broken. If I can pinpoint anything that unraveled after, it's this event. A sexual assault that "didn't happen to me" occurred. Unfortunately, this is common, but I was naive and blindsided. The words my abuser said that night haunted me for decades. I was disgusted by my body's betrayal. The seeds of addiction and a lifelong eating disorder were born then and there.

Shame tried to consume me but I stumbled upon rowing that first week of college. I walked on to the team and found an athlete within. I trained hard. I had potential, so I transferred to University of Wisconsin and morphed into an All-American Division 1 athlete training 6 hours a day, competing internationally, soon on track for the Olympics.

The word "elite" had power for me. It meant *"untouchable,"* and I desperately wanted to be just that. I didn't realize until years later that part of my drive for physical power was born from that repressed trauma of my rape.

I was on my path to superstar now, and a blurred nightmare had no place. I stuffed it further down. Drinking to oblivion began. I clung to outward achievements to mask it all.

I sold my first piece of art at 16, won my first national award at 19. I was published by 21. I had international gold medals in rowing by 20, ranked top 25 in the country. An entrepreneur running a private art school by 22. I was on the fast track with big dreams.. If I could just reach that elite status, I would be ok. I would be untouchable.

PTSD has a special talent for getting in the way. Vivid flashbacks surfaced after coming second in a race. To me, second place was failure. My body failing me again. The assault flashed before my eyes. The floor fell out for the first time, but certainly not the last. I dropped out of school to grapple with everything that surfaced and, in the process, I suspended my Olympic dream.

I hoped to return to school after a year. I vowed to stay single and childless, an artist/athlete wholly devoted to her passions.

If you ever want to hear the universe laugh, set rigid plans not aligned with your authentic self.

I tried therapy and medication. It helped just enough. I started Immersion Studios, my first entrepreneurial adventure. It was so successful that I didn't return to finish my senior year. I bought a house and studio, and began teaching children to draw and selling art. I was living the dream, making good money. I thought I was free and clear.

But the flashbacks continued. Looking in the mirror, I saw someone hideous staring back. I was ill-equipped to cope. Too proud to ask for help. Drugs and alcohol were such an easy fix. I worked by day, partied by night. And suddenly I found myself pregnant. Many people work and run companies with a baby in tow, so I decided so could I! Then came the ultrasound at 5 months. Twin heartbeats flashed on the screen. I was in shock. I knew it was too much. Abortion wasn't for me. So I sold my house and moved home with the support of my amazing family.

There is no greater joy than having a newborn placed in your arms. I got two. Beautiful boy/girl twins that rocked my world. For the first time, I sought help to recover from the rape. I wanted to be the best mother I could be, and deep down I was terrified that that trauma would continue to haunt me, and harm them. But as life picked up, therapy fell to the side.

I returned to rowing, met a fellow rower, dated briefly, then sealed the deal. We were married by the time I was 25. Third baby at 26. The entrepreneurial artist spirit was still alive and seeking a landing place but this time, I had to make big money to justify time away from kids because my husband wanted me to stay at home.

My second company, Jessica Breedlove Designs, was born at age 27 but my pattern continued. The dance between outer success and inner turmoil prevailed. And now I was married to someone who couldn't be pleased. No one knew how I was twisting and contorting to gain approval. The energy required to hide my secrets and attain empty validation and money was starting to unravel my spirit. I hid behind our fast paced well-to-do lifestyle. Anxiety, depression, migraines began to plague me so I sought medical help, desperately needing to continue spinning the illusion that I was supermom. My first prescription of Xanax was written. My alcoholism already had deep roots.

By age 32, we had moved 5 times and I had birthed four more

children. Life reached a feverish pitch. We lived in a wealthy suburb of Pittsburgh so image was important, or so I believed. I had a newborn, 1 year old, 2 year old, 3 year old, along with a 6 year old and nine year old twins. Mega Mother to Seven. Owner of a successful art licensing business. Hopeless addict.

I watched in wonder as my children grew and their curiosity and creativity flourished. They were the joy of my life that kept me going. But I was slipping emotionally. It was even more important I keep it all spinning.

Of course, it couldn't be maintained. My business collapsed. I realized I hadn't slept properly in a full decade, just had a series of intermittent naps. I was exhausted.

Two years away from business and I was enraptured by the drawings of my children so at 34, and entirely by accident, I started Kids Art 2 Canvas, an art company based on celebrating and transforming kids art into large-scale paintings.

Within months I had sold an entire collection to a pediatric office. I was soon solo-exhibiting in a local gallery, featured in magazines and doing interviews. I started a therapeutic artist-in-residence program working with kids with cancer at Children's Hospital of Pittsburgh to celebrate their art in collaborative painting. By age 36 I was coached and primed to pitch to investors and grow Kids Art 2 Canvas into nonprofit and for-profit branches. I was a keynote speaker at the Global Arts in Healthcare convention. Pediatric hospitals swamped me with requests to design similar programs for their patients. I proved the powerful healing art can bring to a terminally ill child.

But here's the truth. How long can someone keep going when their foundation is so flawed? Some people hit rock bottom rapidly. My path was the insidious drip-torture variety, the kind that preyed on my denial. How could I possibly have a problem when I continued to look outwardly successful?

My heart has always been one to serve and help others. But somewhere, the balance had tipped. I was at a loss to help myself. Too much of me had slipped into darkness. That giant heart of mine couldn't bear to look inward. I felt so selfish for falling apart, for continuing to crack when it looked like we had everything. My children were beautiful, curious and intelligent. But my husband couldn't see my worth. No one could know what a fraud I felt like. I stopped sleeping. I started isolating. I coped badly, battled food and alcohol, my war with pills kicked into higher gear. I was completely alone. The tragedy of my marriage was something I couldn't face and I was cut off from connection in every form.

By 38, things spiraled further. My dad was diagnosed with stage four lung cancer. He was my hero, I couldn't bear the thought of losing the only safe man in my world.

Two months later we embarked on a two year journey with our 15 year old to discover that he was positive for cystic fibrosis and congenital lobar emphysema. I stopped painting. All my time was spent in doctors offices. My marriage was in shambles and I saw no way out. A week after I turned 40, my dad died. I couldn't swallow enough pills to numb this kind of pain. By 42 all I wanted to do was die. I almost got my wish. Just before I turned 43, I tried to overdose.

On January 31, 2018 I entered in-patient rehab. It was the first time I came to a full stop in 20 years. No kids, no husband, no phone, no business, no known comfort. But there was rest and safety. I didn't have it in me to pretend. I was raw. The reality of my life took shape as my head cleared and the drugs left my system. I couldn't recall much of the last two years, and that shook me. I found art therapy, meditation, music, healing.

My story is NOT uncommon. I am not unique. Look around. Look closely at those you think you know best. And the ones you don't. Is there light in their eyes? Do they sparkle and dance? Or has the light gone out?

I took baby steps. Broken and raw, I cried like I've never cried in my life. I left my marriage. I began the hard journey forward in recovery. I clung to hope. I stayed sober, but the demons still chased. Remove alcohol and pills and the pain of breaking my family was visceral. Seeing my kids only half time now and living with the pain of hurting them, I ached to numb the pain. Instead, I stopped eating.

Luckily, the seeds of hope were planted, so I didn't back down.

I swallowed my pride. Admitted, "yes, this, too" and entered in-patient treatment to heal the eating disorder.

Facing towards the light takes courage. Making hard choices to make REAL personal change takes strength. Perseverance.

Vulnerability. Humility. Trust. Faith. I didn't do it alone. Asking for help was one of the hardest things for me to do.

It's been a tough road back. I've utilized every modality possible to ensure I never lose myself again. I've gone back to fan the flames of the inner child. I play, I dance, I delight in the intangible precious moments spent with family and close friends. I slowed down. I took accountability for my mistakes, forgave myself, let go of the shame and the guilt. I forgave my past. I stopped playing small and started dreaming big. I shifted my mindset to one that knows in my soul that I am deserving of abundance.

I meditate, journal, paint, stay in therapy, stay connected to my tribe, and stay open to unlimited possibility. I focus on the silver linings in every difficult experience. I avoid the things that harmed me. I set boundaries to protect myself and stay out of conflict, away from toxic people, and anything that threatens my optimism. When it comes down to disappointing others or disappointing myself, I no longer disappoint myself. I did that for far too long.

My creative work is the bravest act of expression that I can make. It is the bravest form of self-care I can practise. And it is my bravest acknowledgment of my unique and authentic spirit that is worthy of this work. It is my bravest act of self-love. And because I've found that, I can give it to the world. I teach others. I host live workshops, online courses, coaching, speaking, writing, sharing. I'm building my dream team to put more good into the world. To reach people that need hope. We can overcome and thrive.

Strategies for success:

Taking **action** has been the absolute foundation of the rapid success happening with Jessica Hughes Fine Art and The Art of Your Story.

These are the strategies I use to keep myself clear, efficient, productive, and brave enough to claim the abundant life that is meant for all of us.

Future gratitude lists and the power of an abundant mindset

Radical Trust has been the superpower of my business. I practice it daily in the form of future gratitude lists. Everyday, I take time to reflect. I focus on the biggest things I need in the near future to help me flourish. I am very specific.

81

I write everything I desire for the future in the form of gratitude using **present tense**, as if it's already happened. I visualize it. I feel it. I write it down. The brain doesn't know the difference between a visualized memory and a real memory.

Take a moment and imagine slicing into a lemon and biting into it. Does your mouth squinch up? Do you feel the sour hit of the juices squirting in your mouth? It feels real. Your brain believes it.

Now imagine money abundantly flowing to your bank account. Imagine vividly how it feels, the rush of elation. Now write down your gratitude for it in present tense. Continue moving down your list. Dreaming, visualizing, and leaning into what it feels like for those things to happen to you. Capture that gratitude and write it down. Do it daily for 30 days, and prepare to be amazed by how rapidly things change.

The fusion of meditation, journaling and art

Meditation puts us in touch with our inner selves. It is a safe space to become conscious of thoughts and feelings and allow them to pass without judgement. After a lifetime of inner-criticism and feeling judged by others, it's been super important and highly impactful for me to find a sacred practice to slowly but surely turn off the inner-critic. To find my intuition again and listen to it.

After meditating, I go straight into stream-of-consciousness writing. 20 years ago, I read Julia Cameron's, "The Artist's Way, A Spiritual Path to Higher Creativity". I have adopted her morning pages ritual. There is so much freedom in spilling three full pages of stream of consciousness writing, so different from a traditional journal. Here, the pen touches paper and doesn't lift until my illegible writing is complete. Three pages full. I don't cross t's or dot i's, and I never reread. It clears my head of all the minutia swirling within. It's my safe space to unload anything I'm repressing.

From there, I've learned that painting, doodling, experimenting with mixed media and different tools on TOP of the writing makes the journaling even more powerful. It covers my words so I am free to write my deepest inner thoughts. Prying eyes can't read what I've written if it's covered and it allows for the nonverbal emotional nuance to be captured and reflected back. Words are effective and powerful, but they have their limit. Shifting into the nonverbal, right brain realm gives the sequential left brain a break. Flow can be achieved through art; peace can be found.

There are many artists using this fusion of modalities, and many more "non-artists" who have found the therapeutic value in practicing this as a tool for wellness. Still intimidated? Reach out to me and I will guide you.

Invest in yourself and your business and network, network, network:

As an entrepreneur, I am the engine of my business.

The more I invest in myself and learn from others who are achieving what I desire, the more powerful the engine is.

I went out on a limb and started my company with zero working capital, so it was critical I really used all the tools available to me. I have maintained that radical trust that if I'm meant to do this work, the funding will appear and it has.

I adopt a mindset of abundance in my decision making. I make decisions like I am a fully funded CEO. Fear has no place anymore.

I've invested in mastermind programs, branding and strategy courses, as well as PR programs that I know have been successful for others, even when I couldn't afford them. I learned quickly that the ROI comes back multiplied when I fully invest in my business. So I commit to being fully present and I do the work to get everything out of what's offered.

Hire help before you're ready

Many creative entrepreneurs run solo companies. But looking hard at the abundance of my dreams, ideas and platforms, I need a dream team.

I map out on paper all the roles I could delegate to take my company to the upper level of what I wish to achieve, and allow this working document to evolve and change as my business grows.

I focus on the things that only I can do, and recognize that there are many people that are gifted in areas where I may be capable but they can do it better and faster. I don't want to be the bottleneck to my growth by trying to do it all.

So I put on that CEO hat, embody the fully funded mindset and begin to hire out help, well before I feel I'm financially prepared to do so. I love employing people to share my mission. It enables me to stay in the joy and stay with the energy that fuels the entire company.

Do what I do best, and hire the rest.

I did it, and you can absolutely do it, too. If you feel called to a purpose, no matter the hurdles, where there's a will, there's a way.

The biggest and most important thing I've learned in this wild life ride is that it's essential I dig into finding my gifts and claiming them. Owning them. Finding the self-worth and confidence to embrace what is unique and special within. No one but me can find my worth and have the audacity to chase my dreams. I strive to heal on the inside, never repress pain, and live so my words and actions are in alignment.

Hope is always around the corner, never lose sight of it. And if you're struggling personally or in business, seek the help to find the answers you are looking for. Believe in your ability to continue.

Failure doesn't exist, it's just an opportunity for more growth and learning. Pain is part of life but the metaphor for everything I do is to turn that pain into beauty. Find silver linings in every darkness. There is room for all of us to succeed and thrive. Own your superpowers and take action.

About the author

Jessica Hughes - abstract painter and therapeutic art expert - uses her triple decade experience as a professional artist, entrepreneur, and mother of seven to help spark magic, joy, and inner transformation through the healing power of art. Jessica Hughes Fine Art is her fourth company. Early in her career she licensed her art for home decor and gift products. She is mom to seven kids and built her third company around the celebration of kids' art. She designed and implemented an artist-in-residence program at Children's Hospital of Pittsburgh for terminally ill children. This program fully encapsulated the healing experience art can bring to the soul.

Jess's fine art painting practice is an intimate emotional exchange between her intuition, vibrant paint and canvas. Her award-winning work paintings and prints are in high demand by collectors worldwide. She is a media-featured expert on podcasts, news and TV. She offers destination workshops, online art and wellness courses, corporate events and is a much-sought-after motivational speaker.

Website: www.jessicahughesfineart.com, www.jess-hughes.com, www.theartofyourheart.com

Facebook: www.facebook.com/jessicahughesfineart

Instagram: www.instagram.com/jessicahughesfineart

Email: Jess@jessicahughesfineart.com

Jessica Perle

Where it all started

This isn't a story of how I grew my business and became super successful within it. This is my story of how I went from giving up on everything to having the drive to even *begin* to start my own business. Because that is the true story of my success!

Here I am, back after investing $20k (aka all my savings and some debt too) into creating my own business. And I'm still alive.

I'm making what may seem like a very obvious statement, but two years prior to this point I did not think that would be the case. Was I in hospital? Nope. At home dying of an incurable disease? Nope. I was just done. Done with my job, my string of abusive relationships, my life and the entire bloody world. I had reached my lowest point, sat on the couch, living back at my ma's and reading *Eleanor Oliphant Is Completely Fine.* I put the book down. I was crying but I was quite calm. I then began to think about how I could end it all. This was my second experience of being suicidal, however the first time was a fleeting encounter and had scared the sh*t out of me. The second time was so different. Reflecting on this second time, when I was calm, cool and collected, this scares me so much more now. The thought of ever going back to "that place" has caused me many a sleepless night.

Now, obviously, I am here writing this for you to read, so I clearly didn't follow through on any of those thoughts. When I look back on that broken woman, I am so proud of myself and how far I have come. It wasn't easy - there was no magic pill (although there was medication) and I had to face a lot of issues I had been avoiding for many years. I describe her as a broken woman as that is exactly how I viewed her. Broken and smashed into tiny pieces. Someone who couldn't put herself back together, nor accept the help of somebody else. After years of mental and emotional abuse from those who said they loved and cared for me, I had a very low opinion of myself. I had lost all sense of who I was, what I liked and what I didn't like. I had felt like this for years. J.K. Rowling's depiction of depression is spot on - I had my very own dementor who chaperoned me wherever I went, slowly sucking the happiness and life right out of me until there was nothing but an empty shell left of what was once a bubbly, confident and outgoing girl.

I am also extremely grateful to the people around me who supported me through this journey. In particular my ma and a couple of close friends, without whom I know I would not be here.

I have always been a problem solver, I love puzzles, riddles and helping others figure out how to work through their issues. My skills in problem solving had a large part to play in getting from that broken woman to where I am now. I discovered how resilient, stubborn and resourceful I could be by going on this journey. I have learnt so much about myself and about others around me too. The last skill (if you would call it that) which helped me grow, is being open to new things - ideas, views, ways of doing things. The list is endless.

The challenge

I used to be an incredibly driven teacher of Maths in a secondary school with a fiancé, house and three beautiful cats. I believed that to succeed I needed to give my all - I had to be busy all the time and I had to be perfect: the perfect teacher, employee, daughter, fiancée ... you get the idea. I was running myself into the ground with unrealistic expectations of myself and constantly striving for the next thing. On top of this, I had made some decisions I wasn't proud of and I constantly punished myself for it. I battled with my mental health for years, resisting a diagnosis and ploughing on thinking *"if I could just get bla bla bla, I'll feel better."* Unfortunately there was always something else I needed to get or achieve to feel better. I remember feeling so desperate to just feel happy and content. I had been promoted, changed schools with another promotion, bought my own house, had a nice car and somebody to come home to at night. So why wasn't I happy?

After admitting what I thought was defeat, I started seeing a psychologist. Sixteen weeks of hour hour sessions later I felt stronger in terms of my self-belief and confidence. After reflecting, I decided that my current situation was not right for me anymore, so I left it all - my house, relationship and my three cats. I moved back to my ma's and was sleeping on a toddler blow up bed in my old high school bedroom.

I'd love to say it was all up from there. I definitely thought that I had done the hardest part but I was so wrong. Four months later was that moment I was on my ma's couch, calmly figuring out how to end it all. It was just all too much. Too much pain, too many emotions, too many thoughts. I wanted out now thank you very much. As I explained before, there was no drama, no hysterics, I had just made my mind up that I didn't want to be here anymore. With support from my ma, I went back to the doctors and this time came away with a high dose of medication, a sick note for work and was put on another psychologist's waiting list.

Fast forward a year past the horrific side effects from the medications, some more counselling and quitting my job with a bully of a boss, I'm in a different part of the country, away from my ma and everyone I know, in a new job and listening to a new podcast. Why is the podcast significant? Because it completely changed everything for me. I had stumbled across this podcast whilst walking through the nearby country park. The content instantly resonated with me and I found myself applying what the no-nonsense woman was saying to my own life. I had found life coaching. Prior to this, I thought life coaching was for pretentious people with more money than they knew what to do with, but this style of life coaching really wasn't like that at all. I was finally starting to learn the tools to get a hold of my life.

I always knew that I wanted to "make a difference". As a kid I was adamant I was going to be a vet. This continued all the way until I was 17 and in college, when I began my first abusive relationship. I had no idea that it was abusive at the time but he was my first ever boyfriend and I gave him everything - I mean *everything*! A year and a very messy break up, death threats and a very broken heart later, I was a mess, failing in college and totally out of love with education.

It took two years to bring me back into education at university. This time, I was going to save the world from climate change one animal at a time. A couple more abusive relationships and some other mental trauma later, I had finished university with a degree in wildlife conservation. At this time, I was engaged, moving was not an option and there were no jobs available in the conservation sector within a reasonable commuting distance. That's when I decided I was going to make a difference by becoming a teacher. Educate the future of this world. One year in I realised that, as teachers, I had no freedom whatsoever. The curriculum served nobody, schools were judged on criteria outside of their control and much more, but this is not a story about how messed up the British education system is.

I still wanted to help. That's where life coaching came in. When I first dreamt up the idea of becoming a life coach and starting my own business, I had so much drama in my mind. Here's an example of one inner monologue:

Brain: so YOU want to be a life coach?

Me: Yes

Brain: Have you looked at your own life lately?

Me: Exactly, I have experience in ...

Brain: Who would come to you for help with their life?

Me: I'm sure there are ...

Brain: Who would PAY for that?

Me: Shit ... you have a point!

Brain: Exactly, you might as well stay where you are. Here is safe. We know here. Change is dangerous. We could die!

So, after some serious work on my beliefs of inadequacy, credentials and my past, I signed up to become a life coach and I LOVE it!

Do I still have negative thoughts?

Yes.

Do I still doubt myself?

All the time.

Do I think I'm going to fail and fall flat on my face with no money to my name?

Abso-f*cking-lutely!

So what's the point?

I now know that I can figure out whatever life throws at me. I have the tools to work through, process and move on from any difficult experience, whether that be emotional, personal, educational or logistical. I can figure it out.

The nitty gritty

I decided to push forward with starting my own business before completing my accreditation for life coaching, as the life coaching business is not moderated by anybody; you do not officially need credentials to work as a life coach. My initial efforts in my business yielded nothing! I was scheduled from 6am to 9pm every day. Working full time as a teacher, working towards my certification, coaching myself and starting my own business. I was so busy and I had nothing to show for it. It was incredibly disheartening. I had no idea what I was doing as I had been off social media for six years at this point and everything had changed. The self-doubt hit me hard. The negative voices of boyfriends past were constantly in my head. My own negative self-talk was super strong too - something I named "the little b*tch in my head." Catchy, hey? This was my first and constant challenge to overcome.

In a world full of instant gratification - hello, Just Eat, social media, blue ticks and binge watching Netflix - I had to learn to be patient. I had to learn to be a beginner again - not my favourite! I was incredibly frustrated with myself and had constant *"I should"* thoughts rolling around my mind - something we'll get into later.

The overwhelm and confusion was, well … overwhelming. I became stuck in this spiral of negativity and lack of confidence. I would then throw in some added pressure of, *"I want to help people and the longer I'm stuck here, the less people I can help."* I began to doubt myself daily. Telling myself that it shouldn't be this difficult; that if I was supposed to be doing this, it should be easy. I thought about just working for another company as a life coach so many times. Maybe I could get a job working for these other fabulous women who clearly have something I didn't.

Giving up would have been easy as I'd have had much more free time and energy. But I'd have also had so much less joy. I had to give it time and I had to put the work in. I had to put myself out there and truly believe in myself - something I hadn't done since I was probably in primary school. This was going to have to go deeper than just doing daily affirmations in the mirror. I was going to have to do the nitty gritty thought work. This was scary but this? This I could do. So, that's what I did and is what I'm still doing - the nitty gritty. The hard work. Showing up for myself every day.

Opening up

I mentioned before that problem solving helped me get out of my rut. I'm sure you're wondering how loving to complete Sudoku got me from suicidal to starting my own business. Well, remember all those tiny broken pieces I had been smashed into? Learning how to put them back together again became my new puzzle. I was a problem to solve and I was the only one who could. I realised that it wasn't that I couldn't put myself back together like I originally thought, I just didn't have the head space to do it at first. Once the threats, control, manipulation, gas-lighting and head f*ckery had broken me up into the smallest of pieces, I could begin again. I began by identifying what was hurting me more. Who or what is the toddler coming in and picking your jigsaw up and breaking it up into pieces again? At first I changed a lot of circumstances but I quickly realised that my brain, my broken pieces would follow me wherever I went.

This is when I began thought-work and realised that I could only control my thoughts and nothing else. At first I had lots of little breakthroughs and it felt amazing. I loved life coaching and thought-work. But that was only the edges done on my personal jigsaw. The next part would be much trickier. I'd have to draw on every ounce of resilience to keep going with this. I'd hit my core beliefs and was now starting to question what my whole outlook was based on. My foundations were rotten to the core and needed replacing before the whole thing (me) came crashing down.

My first major breakthrough happened whilst I was watching a coaching call and a client said something along the lines of, *"it's not fair that they get to go on with their lives and I'm here broken and need to fix myself"*. Oh wow, could I relate! Our coach asked, *"what if you don't need fixing? What if you're not broken?"* Holy Sh*t! This blew my mind. I'd been running around with this whole victim mentality and trying to build on that. No wonder I was still struggling. Being open to different views and ideas has been crucial in helping me move on from the abuse and heal from the trauma. If I hadn't been open to new ways of thinking, I would never have made a start on my business.

The steps

Here are just a few of the steps I took to help me get from my rock bottom to where I am today.

1. Ask for help

If you are struggling in any aspect, be it mentally, personally or in your business, ask for help. Somebody will have the answer, wisdom or knowledge. There is absolutely no shame in asking for help. People see it as a weakness but they are so wrong. It takes some serious strength to reach out - usually to a complete stranger such as a doctor, psychologist or a coach - and say you need help. This help could be in the form of therapy, medication or lifestyle change. Remember that mental health is a serious condition and not a weakness on your part. One description of it is that there is a chemical imbalance in the brain. Would you think a diabetic is weak for not being able to balance their own insulin levels? I'm guessing not. It's a similar concept with mental health. So, if you are struggling your first step is to reach out to somebody for help.

2. Write

Thought downloads are now a part of my daily life. All you have to do is give yourself a set amount of time, start small with only a minute or two then build up, and write down every thought that goes through your head during that time. That's it! Just write down all of your thoughts. At first it will feel totally unnatural. My brain went to *"blank"* or *"I have no thoughts,"*initially. Your brain hates having a light shining on its inner workings. We are so accustomed to letting our brain do its thing that we aren't aware of the thoughts that are going on in our head. Even worse, how damaging those thoughts can actually be. The first step to mental strength is observing what is going on in your own head. Once you have practiced this skill I'm sure you will be surprised at what you find going on in there. If you really struggle with this, like most people do, try giving yourself a focus to begin with. For example you could focus on your business. Think about your business and write down all the thoughts that are coming up for you about your business during the time you have set aside.

3. Routine

Create a strong schedule that you can manage and stick to. This second point is important. There is no point creating a crazy busy schedule which leaves you more exhausted than if you winged it. When suffering with a mental health condition, making a decision can be difficult and incredibly draining. Having a set routine in place can significantly decrease your mental fatigue. This gives you more energy to spend on things you enjoy, like creating your own business. Don't start big though! Time block for all the things that have to get done and then include new things to nourish your life. This is not a tool to berate yourself with if you don't get everything done that you had planned. It's just a way to decrease the amount of decisions you need to make about food, chores and maybe even clothes.

The three steps I have mentioned above have the narrative of mental health as this is my experience, however they are easily applicable to building a business or overcoming any obstacle in your life. They are all part of my lifestyle now, although there are times when I slip into bad habits. This is absolutely normal so do not punish yourself for that. Just acknowledge it then pull yourself back into good habits as soon as you can.

So there it is, a brief overview of my story. It's wasn't pretty and it's not even that pretty now, but that's what I would like you to take away from this. *"Perfect"* is bullsh*t. *"Ready"* is a lie. Perfect and ready drove me to suicidal thoughts. You may not resonate with the mental health side of the story but if you are reading this, you will surely get the link to building myself and building a business as it's the same thing. You have to be healthy before your business will be successful. The skills you need to build a business are exactly the same as the skills I used to build myself. Resilience to keep going, trying new things and learning from each failure. Open to help, learning, and other ways of doing/thinking. Solving problems and not giving up at the first hurdle. After all; it's meant to be difficult. Otherwise everyone would do it naturally. Put your product or service out there into the world and improve based on what the world throws back at you.

Act now, don't wait until you feel ready because you never will.

Don't wait until it's perfect because that doesn't exist.

About the author

Jessica is a mental health and wellbeing coach. She helps women in high-pressureD careers who are being held back either by their own thoughts and beliefs or due to suffering with anxiety and/or depression. She offers 1:1 coaching packages to help her clients go from burnout, overwhelm and anxious to energetic, confident and resilient. Her goal is to help women so that they don't end up in the desperate place that she once was.

Facebook:
www.facebook.com/profile.php?id=100054805624950

Email: info@jessicaperlelifecoaching.co.uk

Mia Belle Trisna

How it all started

They say it's easy to judge a book by it's cover, but I'm telling you the cover of mine is nothing like what's inside..

I fell in love with football by playing it on the streets with boys from the neighborhood when I was eight. Out of curiosity, I ditched my dancing practice, which I had started at the age of five, and joined a women's and a girls' football team five years later. Football became something that defined me within months. I wanted to be the next star, the next future talent. I had a burning desire to become one of the best players. I wanted to be like the greats. Then at the age of 14, my genuine and naive heart was taken advantage of by one of the men's team coaches at my local club. "I'll turn you into the next Marta" and "your dreams can come true with me" were all it took for this little girl to give up her innocence and self-worth. "Just do as I say and everything will be okay" he said, as he laid his hands on my body in a dark parking lot by the forest on a summer evening. At the time, I didn't know what sex even was or that men can take advantage of little girls. He made me feel like I wouldn't achieve success on my own, so my freedom and independence were taken from me. I still regret not talking to my parents about what happened that night. I was too ashamed and I thought I'd make them proud one day if I just listened to his advice and did whatever he told me to do. What I didn't know then was how many years of suffering, pain, lies and being someone else's toy were ahead of me. All for my big dream…

I put aside every piece of dignity and self-love I had to make others proud of me. My parents had just divorced less than six months ago, so a part of me thought maybe my success would be a way to bring the family back together again - to feel happy again. I was broken, vulnerable and that man chose the right moment to prey on me. What I'd give to experience the same teenage years as my friends - playing, having fun, without a worry in the world. Instead, I was told what to do, what to say, and who to be, just for his pleasure. All I had were blank spaces instead of good memories for seven years of my teenage life from trying to forget the trauma I went through. I lost my friends, I lost my happiness and I lost my true self. I had to be strong and act as if I've got it all under control, but behind the scenes I was crying myself to sleep, blaming myself for what was happening and hoping it would all just end one day.

In July 2014, it almost did. I tried to take my life because I was afraid of what people would think of me if they found out the truth. I realized that while trying to be strong for others, I had pushed aside all of my feelings and slowly killed myself inside.

For years, my classmates, teammates and coaches had been spreading and believing rumors about me being with that man voluntarily. I was made fun of and talked about behind my back, no one taking the time or the effort to actually ask me what was going on or believing my words. I felt extremely lonely and sad. All I wanted was someone to really notice and help me. I was constantly lying to my family about where I was and skipping all my friends' parties. I didn't get to do things that I enjoyed - I hated my life.. The only thing that kept me going was the chance to fly to the furthest place in the world for university. I received a full scholarship offer abroad thanks to football - perhaps the only time my dream saved me.

My story came to light during my first semester at college in the United States. I felt ashamed that I'd betrayed my parents and lied to them for so long. I was seeing therapists multiple times a week for a year, just to get to a place of telling what happened without crying and shivering. Coming back home disgusted me - I was scared to visit my family in case that man tried to find me again. And he did. I tried going to the officials but they did nothing. To them, I was just another girl trying to say she had been sexually abused and mistreated by her coach. So I lived my life in fear and shame. Nobody listened to me, nobody saw the real issue, so I thought my voice and my story didn't matter. That I didn't matter.

It happened all over again when I wanted to play professional football in Europe after graduating from university. At first I was so happy to follow my dreams and finally become a professional football player; it was only later I discovered that what seemed perfect at first was, in fact, the darkest place I've ever been to.

I was given my own car and apartment - everything I had dreamed of having - but then put in a situation from which there was no escape. Drugs, alcohol, violence... anything horrible you can think of, I've seen and experienced it all.

What I saw with my own eyes - what I had to go through and what I was forced to do... if you think of a really intense, dramatic action movie that was pretty much my life. I was beaten. I was mistreated. I was abused. I was pushed down lower than the dirt and taken advantage of sexually, mentally and physically. I was disowned by my new team because of having to follow a certain man's rules for me. He owned the whole system, so it was up to him to decide for my life. I was put in a cage. Literally. I couldn't go outside unless allowed, I couldn't hang out with my teammates apart from when necessary. He deleted my social media accounts so I had no one to talk to. I was so cut off from the world and who I was that I actually let him mold me into the person he wanted me to be. He would have nightmares - hallucinations of people coming to get him that would make him psychotic. It made me feel sorry for him, even though he would take it out on me. I fell in love (or so I imagined) with a man who could've turned on me at any second, shot me and dumped my body somewhere in the woods. That really was the lowest I have ever felt, ever been or ever will be. I wanted to die.

This time something told me I needed to survive. I think it was part of the bigger mission I was put on this Earth for. So a few days before they had planned to kill me, I escaped.

113

This is why I want to share my story - I don't want any other woman to go through what I did. This is what keeps me going every day - standing up and being a role model for girls and women like me who didn't have a strong upbringing or sense of self and so sought love and validation from places they shouldn't. Instead of being taught about self-love and educated on sex and relationships, we learned it the hard way. So football ruined my life, but it saved it too because I am here today to tell you my story.

I had to become a new person in every single sense. I've completely rebuilt myself and my life and I want my story to make a difference in someone else's life. Yes, I have wished I could take it all back. I have wished I could rewind time to the day in that parking lot when I was 14 and didn't stand up for myself, because this time I would. But I can't and I don't want to anymore. Because if I hadn't been through all this, I wouldn't be who I am today. So even when I feel tired or I doubt myself, I look deep inside and I know I must push on because I want to save other women from that pain and suffering.

These men tried to bury me, but they didn't know I was a seed. A seed of light. A seed of hope. A seed of love for the rest of the world.

The breakthrough

After escaping the situation, I had to completely restart my life at the age of 25 and it was a very challenging period. I was in severe depression, recovering from complex PTSD, with no idea of who I really was underneath all of this, after all these experiences.. My past was *"erased,"* I felt empty and lost. What now?

Without anyone to tell me what to do, who to be or where to go, I struggled to know what I wanted. I had to shift from being an athlete to joining the workforce. I didn't have a lot of experience in the corporate world, but what I had was what football gave me - willpower, determination and work ethic, as well as the strength, courage and survival skills my past had taught me.

I worked as a director's assistant and then as an office manager to earn enough to pay my bills and have money for food. That's what many of us are told to do by older generations: get a degree, get a 9-5 job, get married, have children, work and retire... and that's pretty much it.

But a year later I was still feeling unhappy and lost with no dream or goal that I wanted to strive for. Deep down I found myself thinking, *"there must be more to life than this."*

I've always felt this urge to help others and make the world a better place, but I never knew how. Until April 2020. I was ill in the middle of Lockdown and I realized that I was just so sick and tired of being a victim of my past, blaming everything and everyone for my unhappiness and letting others control my decisions. I decided it was time to finally create my own dream life.

I joined women's communities online, I met and spoke to women that had been through similar experiences and I realized I wasn't alone. That so many women out there are going through the same things but no one really talks about it. It taught me that maybe what I had been through was just to prepare me for what's ahead. That maybe my experiences are what could help others; maybe my story will be what saves another woman from the same path.

I'd heard the phrase, *"everything happens for a reason"* over and over and, at first, I thought it was insane - why would anyone have to go through this struggle and hardship? I wouldn't wish this on anyone. Finally, it made sense. Maybe we're all given the strength to go through what is placed in front of us so that we can grow, learn, and be better humans.

When we witness the dark and still choose the light despite it all... well, what if that's our superpower?

So I chose to dive all in to do the ugly work - the inner healing from all this trauma and hurt. I hired a coach to guide me through the process - I knew I'd first have to fill my own cup before I could fill others'. I had to learn how to love myself, how to be proud of myself, how to feel grateful for what I have. I worked on my mindset and my healing every day. I decided that in order to help other women, I needed to learn the tools and techniques, read and educate myself on how I could best serve them. Most importantly, I had to learn to lead myself before I could lead others. That's when I understood the power of mastering the self.

It's not an easy path to take when others around you don't know your story, don't see your vision, don't understand why you're doing this. In the beginning it can feel very lonely. It can be easy to compare yourself to other people's success on social media, it can be discouraging to keep going if you're not seeing results immediately and it can be very hard mentally to take this brave step in your life when people around you are judging your choices. But let me tell you.. it all pays off. It's all worth it. At the end of the day, it's your life and no one else's. Why not enjoy it and do what you love? You deserve all that you desire and all the hard work you've put in is noticed and acknowledged and is going to come back to you tenfold. Once I really began focusing on going inward - putting myself first, loving and accepting myself, aligning to my highest self through meditation, visualization, embodiment and many other tools, learning about the Law of Attraction and how the Universe works, things began to take magical turns...

Fast forward to now and it's been two years since escaping; eight months since making that decision to change my life and here I am... shivering with excitement, jumping for joy and crying with happiness in my living room. I can't believe this is all actually happening for me. I've just started my very own coaching business and all my dreams on my vision board are beginning to come true. I feel grateful just to be alive today. One brave decision to fight for my life, to survive, has brought me to this very moment. I feel proud of myself for not letting them win, for picking myself up and turning my life around when it would've been easier to give up. Now I've found my happiness, my power, my true self and I'm fulfilling my mission and making the world a better place one soul at a time, inspiring others to rediscover who they truly are and helping them live the life they dream of.

The steps

So how did I do all this? Along with hiring a coach who helped me with my healing and mindset, I will share with you here some of the practical tools that I've been using daily that have shifted my mindset, energy and emotional state. They've had a transformative impact on my life and I'm sure they will improve your life as well. If you stick to these techniques daily and really stay consistent with it, I can assure you, you will feel more at peace, more grateful and joyful, and more connected to yourself and others around you.

1. Practise gratitude

Every morning when you wake up write down five things you're deeply grateful for. It doesn't have to be complex, but what matters is that as you write these things down, you also feel the feeling of gratitude, of truly being thankful for all these things in your life. Then write 5 things you're deeply grateful for that you dream of having or accomplishing, as if you already have them now. Like it's already happened and is now a reality for you. This is called preemptive gratitude. Extra bonus if you do the same before going to bed. Gratitude is one of the most powerful emotional states we can be in, as it increases our ability to notice all the good that's already around us. It elevates your mood and helps you to stay more present throughout the day.

2. Study the Law of Attraction

Learn and research about this as much as you can, about how you can align to your higher self to attract into your life what you deeply desire. Essentially, it's about understanding that at any moment you have the power to create your reality with your thoughts, words, beliefs, and actions. What you give energy to and focus on in your life, will come back to you. Focus on being grateful for what you already have, focus on giving love and kindness to others around you, focus on what you can control. When you find yourself in a situation where you have to make a decision, ask yourself "what would the person I want to be think/say/do/feel in this situation?" This will help you align to your higher self and start attracting abundance into your life.

3. Meditate

This has been one of the most important tools that helped me make a shift in my life. I now meditate every single day, sometimes twice a day. Begin with just five minutes and slowly build it up. You can simply search online for guided meditations or put on some high frequency music in the background - whatever feels best for you. The process will get easier and easier and you'll start to notice the shifts within 2 weeks of doing it consistently. It has helped me calm my mind, stay more present, find more inner peace and improve my focus.

If things are not as you want them to be at the moment, when it seems like it's not possible to achieve your dreams, when you feel like giving up or staying in that unhappy reality to be comfortable, remember that every one of us is struggling in our own way. We all have our stories. We all have our pain. What you can do, is take that pain, take that suffering and turn it into a positive lesson, into your passion, your mission on this Earth. You wouldn't be you if you hadn't grown through what you went through. I hope my story has inspired you to begin taking action to go for your dreams, to put yourself first, to love and fully accept yourself for who you are and to always keep going. The world needs your kindness, the world needs your love and the world needs YOU...

About the author

After going through mental, physical and emotional abuse, Mia Belle made the brave decision to not let these hardships define the rest of her life. She picked herself up and started to create a new life for herself. She worked hard on herself daily, she learned to listen and voice her own needs, protect her energy and stand up for herself. What she found was a deeper level of love for herself and a new mission in life. She is now on a mission to inspire the world to rediscover the hero within themselves and encourage people to be who they want to be.

As a self-mastery coach with certifications in modalities such as Life and Success Coaching, NLP, Clinical Hypnotherapy, EFT and Time Techniques, she creates a safe space for her clients to rediscover who they truly are and find their purpose in life. Mia Belle guides her clients to new levels of self-worth and self-love by teaching them how to use powerful mindset and manifestation tools, because everybody deserves to live the life of their dreams. Her clients go from victim mode to fully embodying their hero within and leaping towards their dreams with confidence and courage. Mia Belle leads by example, showing vulnerable leadership to her clients and inspiring them to connect to their highest selves and become the hero they've always dreamed of.

Website: www.aimforhero.com
Facebook: Mia Belle
Instagram: @miabellecoaching
Email: hello@aimforhero.com

Mia Doerschner

How it started

It was a cool spring morning. As I sat on our porch sipping my tea, I could hear birds chirping around me. Through the trees I could see the sunlight peeking through, a soft breeze making the branches sway gently. I began my morning routine, going over the To Do list I'd written the night before; responding to emails and messages from clients. It was at this very moment, I realized how far I had come.

This peaceful, serene morning is a far cry from where I was just a short time ago. Sitting in my car, palms sweating, stomach in knots. I was terrified simply about the thought of walking into the grocery store. What if something happened? Who would take care of my kids? Could I possibly get in and get out without ANYTHING happening to me?

As these thoughts swirled around my brain, I was paralyzed,

frozen, in my seat. I gave in to the negativity that held me back from so many moments in my life allowing my anxiety to control my every move. Over the years, I thought about all of the ways that I could end it all; stop the pain, avoid the shame, put an end to the misery. Thank goodness I never gave in to the strong pull to end my life like so many others have. However, I only sank deeper into my hole of loneliness, desperation, and fear.

Looking back at my life until now, I am embarrassed at how much I have succumbed to my thoughts. I allowed events that occurred between my mom and me to splinter and deform my mindset as far back as age two or three years old. Being a rambunctious little girl, I ran out into the street and experienced for the first time my mother's rage. That one parental reaction set in my mind a lifelong need to please others, to want her and others to love me and, ultimately, my fear and anxiety about falling short.

Although I had tried therapy to free me of my pain, it wasn't until I got to the root of my dysfunction that I was able to find peace. My road was long and bumpy and there are days when I still want to crawl into the warm comfort of my anxiety. But then I peer into the other room and see my son playing with his little sister and my heart is filled with pride.

I know that my struggles have made me stronger and my pain has given me purpose. My deepest, darkest moments have shown me how to have gratitude for everything in my life - even the thoughts that tormented me - and through that pain I have developed the empathy to help others.

My journey has revealed to me the priceless gift of life and that each experience, good or bad, has value. At that pivotal moment in my life, when the thought of driving my car off a bridge was more appealing than anything else, I could not see that there was another way. I did not expect that my life could be anything other than what it was; filled with fear, excessive worry, and self-doubt.

It wasn't until I threw back the covers and let in the light that I realized that there is more to being me than the negative things I had told myself or the lies that I allowed to infiltrate my thoughts. I am grateful for the path that my life has taken and proud of the efforts that have brought me this far.

I am the mother of two amazing children – a son who is nine and a daughter who is the sweet age of two and a half. They are my world, my light, and my motivation.

Before I started my coaching business, I walked around in a constant state of hypervigilance and sensitivity to my environment. I was on edge, terrified by my own shadow and anxious about every breath. I allowed my thoughts to predict and control all of my actions and every decision acted as a trigger setting my everyday into a tailspin.

In other words, my life was a mess. How could I be the mother that I wanted to be if I was so anxious about making mistakes? Isn't that a part of parenting? Of course, no parent or child is perfect and each day is a learning experience! Parents will make mistakes, have regrets and want more for their children than they had themselves. But, how could I even make those mistakes and learn from them if I second-guessed and questioned every thought and action?

How did I deserve for my children to love me if I could not love myself? How would my children look back on their mother who was incapable of going to a ball game or ballet in "fear" that something would happen? What would their childhood look like if their mother took her own life? I shudder to think about how their lives would turn out with the knowledge that I could not handle even the simplest of things like a trip to the store.

This was the catalyst for my business and my transformation. Although anxiety and depression do not define me, they have made me who I am today. I would not be in the position to help others if I had not walked in their shoes traveling the same road. While I have always felt compassion for others, my struggles empower me to take empathy to a new level. I have been where you are; felt what you felt; worried about what you worried about. I have been at the bottom and I know that there is only one way to go from there. Up!

I was called to help others by the very nature of my life, my thought patterns and my decision to take control. My life's experience has grounded me in the truth, giving me the power to share with others that if I can do it, YOU CAN TOO! I don't regret any of the things that I have been through or the choices that I have made because I know that all of them were foundational in building my character, my strengths and my abilities. It is what I do with these qualities now that determines what I define as success.

Success is defined differently by everyone. You may define success as a high-powered, high-paying job, a fancy car, and a big house. To me, success is living another day to hear my children giggle knowing that I am shaping their lives by my presence, my decisions and my attitude. My battle with anxiety and depression pushed me over the threshold from an ordinary stay-at-home mom to an extraordinary businesswoman, life coach, supporter and friend.

How I created my business

Creating my business was the easy part. The work that had to be done deep inside of myself was the challenge. I had to first face the reality that I was broken. The first step in any recovery or transformation process is to acknowledge that change is necessary. After many years of ineffective therapy, I stumbled across my savior, the one who would finally uncover the depths of my brokenness, the reason for my dysfunction and give me the tools and resources to change my thought patterns. This therapist was finally able to peel back the layers of the onion that made up my whole being. Once I learned that the skills I needed were there all along - just buried deep inside me, I realized that we are all born with our own strengths and abilities to overcome the challenges that life throws at us. This became my calling and my business model to help others find their strength to overcome.

When I came to this realization that I could use my struggles to help others, I found a new lease on life. Why should anyone have to face another day with anxiety and depression alone when I know that there is hope? I am elated to know that my life has a deeper meaning and a bigger purpose. Wallowing in my own self-pity and sadness was counterproductive to the bigger plans that were laid out for me.

The challenges of starting and running a business are the same across the board – no matter the industry, location, or size, businesses all face the same struggles with finances, marketing, employees and customers. It is how you handle them that makes the difference. Will you allow every challenge to take you down or will you rise above it, using it as an opportunity to grow and learn? I used anxiety and depression as my footstool to propel me into my career. I know that if I have been able to overcome this battle, everything else is simply a new day with new possibilities.

Of course, I still doubt my capabilities. I worry about whether or not I can impact the lives of others or make enough money to support my family. The difference now is that I just worry . . . I don't compulsively overthink it or allow fear to rule my life. I no longer let self-doubt and anxiousness prevent me from putting my foot out of the bed in the morning or from ordering food from a restaurant or from taking that giant leap into starting my own business. Do I still get scared? Of course! But I know that that is okay. I use it as fuel to keep pushing me forward - to help others to take that first step toward recovery and living a life that is full of love, purpose, and enjoyment.

My breakthrough did not include fireworks, a marching band, or a parade. Most of my friends and family may not have even noticed that I was different. I do not have any superpowers, nor do I wear a special suit beneath my clothes. I am just Mia on the outside. The process did not happen spontaneously nor did it bring all the fanfare that you might expect when someone discovers their true self hidden beneath mounds of fear and anxiety. But once I was able to let the light shine through, I knew that there was no going back. I had seen the other side. I knew what it was like to live like someone who did not have to deal with the same throes of depression.

The change

My mindset immediately shifted. It was as if I was looking at myself from a position high above, seeing the sadness and worry weigh me down. I felt light and free and enormously powerful as if I could tackle the world. I began to understand the power of positivity and how your thoughts control all of your actions.

Positivity became my inner strength. Each time that a negative thought or fear tried to rear its ugly head, I immediately attacked it with a positive affirmation, a reassuring thought, or an inspirational message. I began to see each decision that threatened to suck me into anxiety as an opportunity to flex my newfound muscles. However, like any muscle in your body, this process required use, practice, and exercise. I needed to use the lighter weights (positive thoughts) to encourage myself to step out of the car. I then added some more weight (spoken affirmations) to walk into a grocery store. Ultimately, I had enough strength to stand tall, using my full body weight, to speak to the cashier about her day or the weather. As with lifting weights, my positivity muscles needed to be stretched, strained and put under pressure. These previously unused virtues had been deep inside of me all along but I had to learn how to apply them to every situation in my life.

The road to recovery was riddled with potholes, setbacks, and speedbumps. But I know that if I had not started the process, I would not be here today to share my journey through anxiety and depression. I was able to remove the band-aid covering my wounds and emerge on the other side to share with others that there is hope, you can have peace and it is possible to live a life of joy and happiness.

The steps

By working with a coach, I was able to not only uncover the root of my depression and anxiety but lay the foundation for my new life as a confident, strong, positive force. I became the mom to my children that they needed and the motivator that now helps so many others. You too can find your inner strength and use your experiences to move you toward the life that you have always envisioned. If I was able to do it, I know that you can too!

But how? I followed several steps that allowed me to change my mindset and achieve the success that I had longed for.

Step 1: Turn your Attention Inwards

As difficult as it may be to block out the distractions and everyday responsibilities, turning your focus to yourself is the first step in your new journey. You may be thinking, "that is the problem. I am always in my head." I can assure you that by turning inward and focusing on the positive rather than dwelling on the negative, you will begin to discover who you are, how your experiences - even the bad ones - have shaped you into the amazing person you are today and how you will use those experiences in the future. Until you identify and address the deep-seated emotions that drive your behavior, you will not be able to move forward and your thoughts will continue to swirl and drag you deeper into dysfunction.

Step 2: Affirm Your Value

Every day that you wake up is a good day. Open your eyes every morning with a grateful heart that you are breathing and able to make your mark on the world. Repeat to yourself, "I am valuable. I am capable. I am powerful." With each affirmation, breathe in the joy that they bring and use this to strengthen your appreciation for life and the value that you bring to it.

Step 3: Change your Mindset

Of course, struggles will come and those deep, dark thoughts will try to creep in every chance that they get. Change your mindset from negative to positive and push those fears out. Drive away the demons that have kept you captive in your own life. Rather than thinking, "what would happen if I go into the store?", envision yourself walking into the store with your head held high, your chest puffed out, confidently knowing that you can and will change your life.

Step 4: Enjoy the small wins!

When you are faced with anxiety and depression, even small things are extremely difficult. Celebrate every small win – you got out of bed this morning and could take care of your children; you called to make an appointment at the doctor's office; you pushed away the negative thoughts that threatened to pull you down; you put one foot in front of the other. No matter how small or inconsequential each thought or event may seem, celebrate it - give yourself a pat on the back, splurge on a coffee or do a dance! With each small step, you are moving closer to becoming the person that you know you can be.

Every morning is fresh and new and will bring its own challenges. Transformation will not happen overnight but with diligence, self-acceptance, self-love and patience, you will overcome your struggles with anxiety and depression as I did. I can help you walk through your journey as a life coach, accountability partner and friend, guiding you to achieve the life that you want. I did it and you can too!

I know and understand the challenges of starting a business. When I decided to embark on this journey, I was excited, nervous, and a bit anxious. The thought of following this path in my life triggered those feelings and emotions that I had worked so hard to control. But I knew that for the sake of my children, my loved ones, and my own happiness, I had to step out of my comfort zone. I had overcome something that many others struggle with as well. I had been at the bottom and knew that there was only one way to go from here: up!

Although you may struggle in your business journey and stumble from time to time, you have the strength within to overcome, to fight and come out victorious as I did. There is a light at the end of the tunnel and by following some of the steps that I continue to use every day, I know that you too will look back at the struggles with pride in knowing that you did not give up.

About the author

Mia is like a light at the end of a long journey. Her struggles with anxiety and depression are not a sad tale of sadness and hopelessness. She was able to use her experiences and trauma to not only overcome the deep lack of self-worth and shame she felt but to propel her life to new heights. Using her cherubs as inspiration and motivation to gain control of the life that was spiraling downward, Mia set in motion a journey which she is still amazed at. As each day unfolds, she stares in amazement at the place that she was compared to the vision that she sees for her future.

By implementing a 4-step process into her daily life, Mia was able to rein in the anxiety and depression that plagued her since she was a teenager. She gained control of her thoughts, affirmed her positive qualities, changed her mindset and set goals for her future. Mia moved from a state of wallowing in self-pity, doubt, and regret considering all of the ways that she could end her life to one in which her light shines like the North Star on her loved ones, friends, and clients. She has shaken off the dirt of her past and used it as a catapult to propel her life and career into an area that she could never have dreamed of.

Now inspiring and encouraging others that they too can fight off the demons of anxiety and depression, Mia is a successful business owner, life coach and mom.

Facebook: www.facebook.com / missmiaofficial23

Email: info@embodiedmindcoaching.com

Miella Ravenscroft

Are you ready to manifest your wildest dreams with ease?

I'm sitting here in my new build dream house. I have just bought my dream car. I have three gorgeous kids and a wonderful husband. I work with my dream clients from all over the world and I make more money than ever working less than ever.

Most importantly, I am happy. Happy with my life. Happy with my business. Happy with myself.

I help female entrepreneurs become Abundant & Badass, become a match for their dream business and earn a sh*t ton of money by mastering their MindBration®, so they can travel, enjoy more freedom, and be their own boss in every area of life and business.

If I had to sum up my life in one word, it'd be: wild. I am the happiest and most authentic version of myself that I have ever been. I love my marriage, my family, my home and my friends. I have an incredible business, and I work with clients I adore. I make a loads of money consistently whilst having FUN. And now I want you to have the same opportunity. To create YOUR dream life from the inside out.

Are you ready?

Let's go!

"What the f*ck is wrong with me?"

"What am I doing here? What is wrong with me? Why can't I just be like everyone else? When will I learn to be satisfied with what life has to offer?"

I'm sitting on a train. I'm on my way to Copenhagen Business School where I am studying psychology and business.

I am looking around at the other people in the train.

They are on their way to work.

"They look like zombies," I think to myself. Nobody is smiling.

142

Their eyes have no spark at all. They look dead inside.

"Is this all there is to life?"

I feel like I can't breath. Like I am trapped on the wrong planet.

"There must be something else. It can't be true that I need to study forever just to get a boring job until I die. There MUST be more to life. Otherwise I am not sure I'll survive it."

I was around 20 at this time and I felt so lost. Like I didn't fit in in the "normal' way of doing life.

Do you know that feeling?

Like you are born on the wrong planet and you just don't fit into "normal"?

Then you are in the right place. Because I want to make this chapter about you! I want to show you HOW you can create your wildest dreams from the inside out by just being YOU (because who wants "normal" anyway).

That's why I'm here to share three powerful steps you can do right away to start manifesting your wildest dreams.

But first...

Zombie life - No way!

Luckily I didn't end up as one of these zombies. Luckily I decided that there WAS another way. I dropped out of business school, started studying psychology at another school and decided that I would be my own boss at some point. Because having someone deciding over me was NOT my thing!

Now, I would love to say it was plain sailing from there but that would be far from the truth. The truth is that it took me three years and two failed businesses before my success started taking off. But then it went fast - I had great fun and great success, money started flowing in. My business took off but something was still off.

I was working way too much compared to how much money I made and about seven years into my business I almost burned out. I had created this job for myself where I pleased my clients but my online social appearance was boring because I tried to be perfect at everything. I tried to show up as the good girl -the girl that wanted everyone to like her. The girl that tried to make everyone happy. The girl that would do everything to make sure her clients got the results they wanted.

I was working 24/7, always online, always being there for my clients. Always trying to please everyone. Thinking I could do better, be better, make more money, sell more.

I had created my own hamster-wheel and it was spinning so fast I was about to be thrown off.

You have a dream life - what is wrong with you?

Looking in from the outside, I was living *"the dream life."* I had three wonderful kids and a wonderful husband. I was living in Bali, I had a nanny, a cleaner and a pool.

But I was done. I had nothing more to give. Up until that point I had been hustling and hustling and giving and giving. Making a lot of money but not being happy. Again, I had all these thoughts.

"'What the fuck is wrong with me? Why am I not happy? Why are my results not matching all the energy I put into my business?

Why the hell can I not reach 6 figures or more?"

I felt so defeated, stuck and like there was something fundamentally wrong with me but instead of taking time off, I kept going. I tried everything on the outside. Changed my products, changed topics I taught, changed my prices... Changed and changed and changed everything in my business. But nothing had changed in me.

I was tired to the point where I had nothing more to give.

I closed down some of my 1:1 clients and shut down some of my products. I hired someone to handle my emails - something I should have done way earlier and...

I let go. I slept. I meditated. When I worked I only did what was absolutely necessary.
Slept some more. Let go of planning. Let go of forcing. Let go of hustling. And then...

I had my first six figure month ($107,000 to be exact) and needless to say I was astonished. I had been trying for seven years and now it had been delivered to me with ease.

Something new was born in me - a realisation that there was

something I hadn't been seeing. that there was another way. I started to see that I could attract money, dream clients and all that I had ever wanted from the inside out with ease.

Then one night, I woke up and heard the word "MindBration®".

My response while almost still asleep was, *"what is that?"* and the answer came immediately: *"everything in your business will surround this word."*

At first, I thought it was silly but, as you might know, when the universe wants you to really *get* something it will not let you off the hook.

Clarity

Suddenly I understood why someone somewhere had given me that word.

It was the answer to why I had struggled SO much during the first seven years of my business but had my first 6 figure month when I let go. I started to realize that manifestation and creating my wildest dreams would require me to align my mindset AND my vibration aka my MindBration®.

I started testing it out in my own life as I always do before I share it with my clients. I needed to see if I could reproduce the results by letting go of my old way of doing things and instead embracing this new approach.

It was A LOT of back and forth for me because my ego constantly told me how stupid I was believing that I could *attract* my clients, money and everything I ever dreamed of by meditating, taking care of myself and raising my MindBration®. I started creating courses around MindBration® and how to attract dream clients, money, confidence and happiness.

And, oh my, did it work!

That year I had my biggest year ever and I only worked seven months out of 12. It was SO easy and SO much fun. The hardest part was actually to let go of my old habits as a client pleaser, raising my prices and just showing up 100% as myself.

It was scary and there were a lot of times when I felt like crawling back into my old way of doing things. *But I knew that this was ALL IN or nothing.*

If this didn't work, I would give up my business so I had nothing to lose. At this point I started seeing all these amazing results. I attracted my dream clients paying my highest prices to date. I had more money than ever, I was happier than ever and I enjoyed my business. I started having more energy again and saying no to clients that were not a match. I had reached a new point in my business where I could create results in an EASY way with a lot of joy and flow.

When I created my first course around MindBration® I was scared as hell that it wouldn't work for my clients but I took the chance. I created practical tools on how to co-create awesome things with the universe. I created tools around how to manifest money, rock solid confidence and more happiness. I created tools that would help them let go of what had been blocking them and tools to reprogram their limiting beliefs. I wanted it to be PRACTICAL and easy to use for everyone.

Forty amazing women signed up for the course and they got AMAZING results. In total they manifested $658,604 in only 12 months. Two women became pregnant. Seven people quadrupled their business income in only two months. Almost all 40 manifested money, happiness, confidence and more ease in their life and businesses.

I was blown away - this stuff actually works. Not only on me but also for my clients. This was the start of a new way of doing business for me.

After living in Bali for three years with my husband and our three kids we decided that we wanted to move back to Denmark. As I write this, I'm sitting in my new build dream house.

I ENJOY what I do today and I have the freedom to do what I want.

And now it's your turn.

I want you to have the most amazing life and business too without all the stress and hustling.

If I told you right now to let go and surrender you would probably be sceptical. I totally get that. Because if you are a hard working high achiever it doesn't feel natural for you to do this. You get a kick out of being busy and creating results and a part of you (let's be honest) only feels good enough when you are creating amazing results whilst working hard.

If it comes too easily you have that feeling of being just lucky or like you've cheated. But, let me tell you, you can have it all and it doesn't have to be hard and take forever. Everything can and will change in an instant when you learn how to raise your MindBration® and co-create with the universe instead of doing everything all by yourself.

That is why I want to give you four practical steps that you can apply TODAY so you also will be able to attract the business success you are dreaming of and a ton of money with ease.

Are you ready? Great.

Let's go.

The steps

1. Know that creating success is 80% MindBration® and 20% doing.

You might ask, *"so what is MindBration® and how do I use it to my advantage?"*

I will tell you right away. I'm quite sure you have heard of The Law Of Attraction. Like attracts like.

That law states that everything is ALWAYS available to us so if there is something we want that is not already in our life, it's because we are not yet a match for it - meaning that you have limiting beliefs (and habits) around why you can't have, do, attract or be something.

Your MindBration® might be set on *"not good enough or lack"* so you will attract more *"not good enough or lack"*.

To tweak this you have to reprogram your subconscious mind by affirming new beliefs again and again. If you have tried affirmations and they didn't work - hold on! Because, as I told you, manifestation is not only about mindset (telling yourself the affirmations) it's also about your vibration (your feelings).

So when you do your affirmations and you are reprogramming your subconscious you also have to ask yourself, *"if I already knew that I was good enough in this moment now, how would I FEEL?"* and then you need to let yourself feel that feeling of already being good enough!

This will make ALL the difference in the world.

Let me give you another example.

You want to attract more clients. What would you say to yourself if you were already that version of yourself that attracts dream clients with ease? What would you feel?

Write it down and start practicing it now. This way you will raise your MindBration® and the Law of Attraction WILL send you new and better things based on what you are emanating now. Because like attracts like - it's a law!

2. It's ALL about self-worth!

I remember when I started coaching. In the early phase I didn't have a niche so I coached people who wanted to lose weight, wanted to have more money, wanted to attract the love of their life and all kinds of things they wanted to create.

Every time someone left the room I'd realise it all comes down to self worth.

And that is still true for me the day today.

When you know you deserve the best then you will attract the best.

So how do you use this to your advantage?

Take out a piece of paper and write at the top, *"If I know that I deserve the best,"* then ask yourself:

What would I let go of?

What would I do more of?

What kind of life would I live?

What would I tell myself every day?

Take your time to answer these questions and then start LIVING it in your life - because if nothing changes nothing changes. You have to be the change.

3. Find someone who has created what you want to create and pay them to show you how you can do the same

For too many years I thought that I needed to figure everything out myself. Heck, I was even proud of being that hardworking hustling girl that would not ask for help. But, oh my…that was not a very good decision.

I could have reached where I am today WAY faster (even though I believe there is a reason for everything) if I had just been willing to invest in myself and had hired a coach or a mentor. I learned along the way that I also need someone to call out my bullsh*t and tell me when I am holding myself back instead of going big.

I learned along the way that I DON'T need to do it all by myself and when I focus on my zone of genius my business thrives and I am WAY happier and more abundant.

Stop doing it all by yourself. Reach out. Find someone (use your intuition) that can believe in you and help you step into The Next Level version of yourself.

You will thank yourself for doing this sooner rather than later.

4. You have the most powerful creator inside of you - don't waste it!

If I could give you one piece of advice, it would be to trust yourself, believe in yourself and use your intuition. You can do WHATEVER you set your mind on as long as you are willing to work on both the inside (your MindBration®) and the outside (the inspired action). Don't waste precious time telling yourself all the reasons why you can't follow your dreams.

You are unique and the world is just waiting for you to step into the next level version of yourself.

The world is just waiting for you to become Abundant & Badass!

About the author:

Miella is the founder of the manifestation concept MindBration®. She helps female service based entrepreneurs become abundant by mastering their MindBration® so they can travel, enjoy more freedom and be their own boss in every area of life and business.

Website: www.abundantandbadass.com
Instagram: Abundant and Badass
www.instagram.com/abundant_and_badass (be aware of the _)
Facebook: The Abundant & Badass entrepreneur by Miella Ravenscroft www.facebook.com/groups/301178137433317
Email: Support@abundantandbadass.com (I would love to hear all the amazing things you are manifesting - don't hesitate to reach out!)

Neeta Hanzra

How it started

"I'm gonna sit down. Don't ask me why but my legs are shaking."

I clearly remember the words I said to my husband six months ago as I get ready today to deliver a presentation to a group of over 80 people.

You see, until that moment where my legs started to shake six months ago, I was living with a 'Misbelief'. Misbelief that in order to achieve a certain type of success, I needed to have a certain type of personality. A personality that I have lost somewhere in the last 10 -15 years of personal struggles.

The very thought of speaking in front of a crowd back then made my legs shake.

I look at what I have now with total 'disbelief'. Disbelief that a girl like me, who had always put others first, can sit in front of a camera and give a presentation in front of potentially 3,000 people. A 'disbelief' that I have raised my prices almost five times in the last six months and people are willing to pay me that much. It still gives me goosebumps.

The journey of these six months up to now was a total rollercoaster of emotions. What took me through these ups and downs was my ability to 'foresee the future' (no, I am not a psychic medium) alongside being able to transcend myself into a feeling of detachment.

Born and raised in India, I came to the UK at the age of 26 almost 15 years ago. Settling into a new family and culture wasn't easy anyway, but add a foreign language (English) to the mix and it was a recipe for almost emotional breakdown.

Trained as a teacher from India, now I found myself training in the grand role of a wife and a mother of three. Just after my daughter was born, I suffered from severe eczema that made it hard even to look after my children and do day-to-day activities.

Hitting rock bottom

When my youngest son was ready for nursery, I decided to go back to a 9-5 job.

I would leave the house at 7am with my three children, drop them off in two different places (school and nursery) and, if traffic permitted, just about have enough time to login to my computer before it flagged me up in the latecomer list.

Often I'd be late to pick up the kids as I couldn't leave a client mid-conversation on the phone. My kids would look at me like helpless kittens through the school office window. The whole thing would make me want to cry.

I always knew there was more to life than the one I was living. I started reading self help books to boost my confidence and create a life that I could live on my own terms. I wanted more time to spend with my kids and financial freedom.

Sitting in my car after another pickup/drop off issue, tears filled my eyes. I was feeling like a total failure as a mother. But then I had this epiphany. Something needed to change. *'How can I be present for my family and still have financial freedom?'* I thought to myself.

My earlier interest in dressmaking took me to personal branding and styling. I hired a social media coach and started marketing myself. As my business was just picking up momentum, the pandemic hit and nobody wanted to even talk about personal styling or branding.

I hit a rock bottom again. But by this time, I had added another feather to my cap: Social Media Marketing. Over the course of three to four years trying to work out how I could create an online business, I had done countless courses and learnt from the industry leaders a thing or two about social media marketing.

As more and more new businesses were coming online, I decided to help them to set their business up on the right foot. All this led me to provide services as a social media manager and marketer and finally a strategist.

Here I realised one more thing. Yes - at surface level, social media marketing looks like it consists of just one component: content. But there are some other moving cogs in this marketing machine and one of them is sales.

In the beginning, my conversion rates were low. It made me doubt my abilities. I was frustrated. People were raving about my content, coming on to the calls with me but not buying. Call after call with no sales and I felt like giving up.

My confidence in my business hit the floor again.

Rising again

But here is where my ability to "foresee the future" helped me to break that barrier. Somebody once said to me, "*if, at the lowest point in your life, you can imagine yourself in a better place,* *you can survive any sh*t life throws at you."*

But how can you see past the present moment when you are pinned to the wall, you may ask.

And this is where the 'detachment skill' comes in handy.

Rather than beating yourself up, in this state you detach yourself and your 'worth' from the current situation and you look at the situation from an objective perspective. From the outside. It helps you understand the situation in a new light. It helps you to ask yourself honestly, *"what went right. What could be improved?"*

Once I could see the situation from the outside, I could see where the problem was.

Now the good thing is, once you know where the problem is, it's easier to fix it. I hired a coach who helped me to refine my sales process and filter out leads, who helped me to create a new mindset around money and show people the value of working with me.

The steps

There were few steps that I took in order to achieve rapid success.

1. Every time I found myself comparing myself to anyone, I stood in the moment and prayed for the universe to give that person abundance and fulfil their desires. It uplifted and purified my feelings towards the things I felt less than or more than (comparison can come in both forms).

2. I stopped hanging out in groups, places or platforms where gossip was the main form of entertainment. You don't want to leak out your energy and time in useless activities.

3. I changed my language. Instead of *"nervous"* I started to use the word *"excited."* Before every major event, I deliberately lifted my arms in the air and said to myself joyfully, *"I am excited to meet people."*

4. I visualised my success every day. To confirm my beliefs, I journaled as well.

5. I invested a lot of money and time in learning a lot of skills but when somebody asked me for help or advice, I never held back on value because nobody ever became poor by helping someone. It makes them wonder, *"if the free stuff is so good what will the paid be like?"*

If you want to achieve rapid success, then believe in the Power of One in your business in the beginning.

Pick up one niche, one ideal client, one platform and one offer. Outline one strategy on a piece of paper and act on it every day. Do the things that need to be done in order to bring in new clients. Minimise all the distractions - phone and household chores, to name two - and give two dedicated hours to your business morning or night.

Follow these steps, stand back and watch it flourish.

About the author

Neeta Hanzra is the founder of Neeta Hanzra Consultancy and the creator of the Intentional Alignment Method. She has worked as the social media manger and marketer for a number of businesses and currently works as a social media coach and strategist at Neeta Hanzra consultancy .She lives in the Uk with her husband and three children.

Website: Neetahanzra.com
Facebook: Neeta Hanzra consultancy
Email: Hello@neetahanzra.com

Rachel Feldman

How it started

I suppose you could call my success rapid, but when it's your heart and soul poured out everyday driving your vision forward, 'rapid' is debatable!

There was a moment a few years ago when I realized I had achieved my goal - beyond my goal. I built a successful business out of a passion for health and wellness, I was earning six figures and supporting my family and I helped other coaches achieve their dreams. It was the trifecta.

I had taken control of the most challenging parts of my life, years of struggling with health issues and created my future. After learning to advocate for myself, I found a passion that helped me heal and set the groundwork for a career assisting other coaches to help their clients. Clients like me whose needs were not fully met. Coaches like me who wanted to drive their business but didn't know where to start.

I have a lot of gratitude for these achievements - appreciation that I keep believing in myself, that I fail forward and that I can find the blindspots. Because achieving your dreams isn't easy and it doesn't happen overnight. I have had to give myself more than one pep talk - dust off my knees after a few falls and find the lesson. I keep my eyes on the horizon and not on the ground, so I can see the opportunities as they come. All of these facets of my personality got me to that moment and kept me reaching for more.

I started my wellness business in 2010, at the height of the financial crash. I had left a lucrative job several years before to focus on family. We had two small children. First, my husband lost his job and then we lost most of our life savings. The stars seemed less than aligned. It was at this point I said to my husband, *"I am going to support us. I am going to make a lot of money as a health coach."* That simple. A decision was made.

Before 2010 I was a commercial real estate agent. I loved commercial real estate. It was a business that centered around meeting and connecting people. I focused on the sales side. I always honed my skills and wanted to make sure I found my clients the right property for them. My favorite clients were always highly committed to creating their vision for their commercial portfolio. I was fully committed to my clients and my reputation reflected that. Potential buyers and sellers took my calls because they knew if I was on the other end of the line, I would have their best interest in mind. I wanted to be as successful as I could for myself and my family - a fact that has always been my *"why."* I keep *why* in mind daily. It guides me and keeps me moving forward. And forward is the only direction worth traveling.

The start of my journey to becoming a health coach was tough.

I wanted to do it because I was so frustrated with my health issues that had started when I was 14. At 14, I was diagnosed with a stomach ulcer. I was put on medicine right away, which I'm grateful for but unfortunately, so many doctors don't have time to educate the family or child about even the basics of changing their diet or taking a probiotic, let alone the steps to heal their gut.

I was 18 years old when I had my first asthma attack. I was put on steroids and codeine cough medicine. My asthma was not getting better and within a few years, it was resulting in monthly visits to the ER. I was even put on life support after one episode.

I struggled to find answers for my health. Many diagnoses and frustrations with the medical system later, I took back my power.

I started researching, asking questions and hiring people who could possibly help me get to the next place in my health journey. I enrolled in Nutrition school at the Institute for Integrative Nutrition. I made a decision to pursue a dream.

When I decided to make health coaching my career, I had limited time as the kids were under the age of four. I knew I needed to learn the basics but so far had only googled, *"how to start a health coaching business."*

I studied people in my industry, my potential niche, watched many Youtube videos and got going. I had no idea what to do, but I started. I got an LLC and registered my business.

Before I share with you my successes, you need to know that going after your dream is one of the most challenging things you will ever do. If it were easy everyone would do it, right?

So much of success is believing in yourself when nobody else sees your dream. I need you to make a declaration today. This second. You will commit to not giving up, even when it gets hard or uncomfortable or even when you fail.

All you need to remember is to fail forward. Any of us can achieve success, as long as we are willing to let go of our old stories, narratives about ourselves and declare we are going to despite our fears.

Where do fears come from, anyway?

Fears are memories. They are the worst case scenarios in our head. They may even come from a parent who felt their anxiety and pushed their fears onto you. Maybe a school teacher told you that you couldn't do something.

Take a few moments to think about the fears and the negative Nancys and Nathans that live in your head. Take a few deep breaths. The only requirement for success is to be willing to redefine your inner critic.

I created a profitable and sustainable business whilst watching many of my wellness coaching friends quit on their dream. But with school fees to pay for and our savings gone, I was committed to making this business a reality.

I committed myself. I dedicated myself to my dreams and my "why".

Yes, I wanted to quit on my dream about 86,400 times a day. There are 86,400 seconds in a day, which means my entire day was filled with self-doubt and fear. I can stand proud and say I pushed past that fear and managed to create a six figure business that supported my family and my dreams.

See, anyone can start a business. Most people have dreams they take to the graveyard or dreams that stay in their minds. For me, this was more than a dream - it was my purpose.

I did not have money to start my wellness business but I knew I wouldn't let anything get in my way. I had a crappy free website. I could not figure out automation for my email marketing. I could not connect a payment button to a sales page or even link my calendar to my *"work with me"* page. I knew nothing but I didn't quit because I was unwilling to give up on a dream of helping people change their lives and making money whilst doing it.

Did I have a special skill set? Was I better at marketing? Was I better at creating value for my clients than another coach? Did I have a special strategy?

The answer is no. I just had a big *"why"*.

Too often, I see wellness coaches quit on their dream. I hear people say things like, *"I tried everything,"* or, *"I just don't have the money to do Facebook ads,"* or, *"I just was so tired marketing on social media."*

I used to have excuses too but I was unwilling to let my purpose and dream go to the graveyard.

You don't need to be an intellect. You don't need to be a business major. You don't need to have nailed tests in school. You don't even have to know how to start a business. If I can share one piece of advice that will help you go after your dreams even when nobody sees them, it would the simple rule I've lived by and spoken about time and again: you need to know your *"why."* This will unlock your feeling of purpose, which is far stronger than a simple feeling of passion.

I created a health and wellness business that allowed me to live my life while fulfilling my purpose. I did not quit because I am clear on why I'm doing it. I had to talk to my future self and remind myself that I could still move forward, even if I was scared.

As I look at where I am today, I'm filled with pride. I get to help coaches who want to change lives and make money doing it. My coaching business's success led me to create another business helping coaches save time and money in order to have more of both to work on their dreams. Today we sell done-for-you content to those in the wellness space. Instead of one coach, we can help coaches change lives worldwide.

Getting clear

If I can do it, you can do it.

There are challenges at every step when you are creating your business. Since I started my business without the money for Facebook Ads, Instagram Ads of Youtube Ads, I had to build my list organically. I struggled with everything from automation to organising my website just like everyone else.

But I knew that if I could get somebody on the phone with me, I would convert them. I have a lot of empathy for people. I'm also good at stepping into a person's shoes so I can understand their opinion.

I knew I would be able to listen to their needs instead throwing an offer down their throat like some of the coaches I had seen try and fail. I created Youtube videos and added my phone number and email to the description.

As I said before, I struggled with time being a mom in her 30's with two kids under the age of 4 when I started my wellness business, but I learned fast to be disciplined so I could make an impact.

I created a schedule for myself with my non-negotiables - the things that absolutely had to get done each week - that involved a strategy for visibility. I had no idea how to blog, let alone create a video, post on social media, or create offers, but I kept thinking about my struggles, kids, and purpose. I was consistent.

Of course, I doubted myself and compared myself to those who had perfect websites and fancy images on their social media profiles. BUT I also knew my ideal client needed me only to have certain things perfected:

- Clarity on their pain points

- A clear message

- Free offers that solved mini issues

- Paid offers that solved big problems

The only special skill you need to have is the commitment to your dream. I was clear on my purpose so let that drive me instead of trying to create the perfect roadmap.

I am successful today because I fail forward. I lean in when most say things like, *"I can't."*

The only person stopping you from showing up consistently,

practicing your message, thinking about your ideal client and their daily struggles and how your ideal client is struggling emotionally, physically, or spiritually is you. It's your own ego and pride.

For many years I struggled and did not have the tools but someone once said to me something that really resonated: *"If you don't show up in this wellness business, you deny your potential client a solution. Think of this man or woman feeling helpless. You were there. This business is not about you. This is about your purpose."*

I have learned to be honest with my fears about not being enough or sounding stupid (all those old stories). When you let go of that fear, you have space for the creative and intuitive flow that is required to build your business. You will start to see endless possibilities instead of a linear approach.

Stop spending time looking for the perfect solution so you have more time to spend thinking about your potential client struggling as you did. Your *"why"* should make you cry.

Here are the exact tools I used to start my wellness business without breaking the bank.

The steps

To build and grow a health and wellness business, particularly in the first few years, can be overwhelming. No business can be started free of cost. Even if it is online, you need to bear the cost of hosting, domain registration, advertisement and all sorts of other weird and wonderful things you probably haven't even thought of yet. But it doesn't mean that the health and wellness business has to be expensive in the long run - you don't need to be rich to start your wellness business; you just have to be smart with your time and money!

I have been practicing in the health industry for many years. Since we lost our savings, I learned how to use free tools to build my dream business. Several free or low-cost tech tools may help you automate processes, promote your products or services better and run your business smoothly, hence saving you time, money, and energy.

There are a large number of tools available in the market so, at times, it becomes difficult to choose the best one. These tools may help you run your business efficiently and seamlessly, whether it's booking clients, filling out forms, adding clients' names to your mailing list or setting up a website. And the best thing is, they're all free.

Below are 4 steps you can take to start your business.

Step 1: Get clear on your purpose

I need you to see your dream. Write it down over and over. Tap into your *"why"* daily. Platforms and technology may fail you at some point but as long as you understand your purpose - that "why" you can rest assured that *you* will never fail you.

Step 2: Define Your Niche

Start by narrowing down your niche to a place that suits your interests, skill set, knowledge and talent AND that will produce a profit for you.

Understand who your clients are – when you can clearly understand who your ideal client is, you will be able to narrow down your niche and business focus even more. Take the following into consideration:

- Gender

- Age

- Income

- Habits

- Hobbies-Interests

- Geographical Location

- Main Health Issue

Why is this information important? Imagine if your ideal market was 40-50-year-old women who have teenage children but your marketing is geared towards 20-30-year-old millennials – your ideal market will not be attracted to what you are offering!

Step 3: Create a website

Every business, no matter whether it's small or large, must create its online presence. And this can be possible only by building a website. Think of your website as your home for your wellness business. You don't need to spend thousands on it - there are plenty of third party platforms you can use instead, all of which will guide you through the process of building a website yourself.

Step 4: Set up your Social Media

No matter if you have a thriving 1-1 or membership or sell courses, you need to be visible. You must make your presence on social media. It helps you to find your target audience easily, promote your offerings to them as well as share content and make the most of SEO. It can help with list building and networking too.

There is never an excuse not to go after your dreams. Too often we think we can't do it because we don't have the money or we don't have money for advertising. I built a six-figure dream business on these free tools, which means you can do it too.

All you have to remember is your *"why."*

About the Author

Rachel Feldman is a health coach and business strategist for wellness industry professionals. She helps new and thriving coaches launch and sell signature offers the easy way with done-for-you programs for every health niche.

Rachel graduated from the Institute for Integrative Nutrition in New York City, Wild Rose Natural College of Healing, the International School of Detoxification and Natalia Rose Advanced Detox Certification Training. She has been featured in Mind Body Green, The Huffington Post, Thrive Global, Forbes, and many others.

After struggling with her own chronic health issues, Rachel turned her passion into a thriving health coaching business. Now she supports other wellness pros in building successful businesses using simple strategies and easy-to-launch programs.

To date, she has helped over 8,500 coaches finally turn a profit, book more clients and save time creating content, allowing them more time to build their know, like and trust factor.

Grab some free tools at rachelafeldman.com and build your biz stat at yourhealthcoachbiz.com.

Sabrina Cochran

How it started

All of this has happened because I refused to allow for my story to be one chapter. I refused to be one label. I came from earning $4.77 an hour to having a $20,000 month in earnings. Breaking generational poverty was the key to my success.

A good friend once told me that, *"You can't gain ground standing still."* And for me that is what I was doing. I was standing still. The stillness provided comfort. It allowed me to stay in a place that, as miserable as it was, felt like home. It provided me with stability. It was the devil I knew. Moving forward with action and purpose was unfamiliar and unknown. It was scary. What if I failed? What if I was judged for the way I looked? What if I was judged for the way I sounded? You get the picture. My mind continued to swirl with negativity. But in all the swirl of negative thoughts, I also began to wonder... but what if I didn't?

What if I could be successful?

I kept thinking of my friend's statement, *"You can't gain ground standing still."* It was the push I needed to gain some control in my life. This started out small. I sought out religion and unconventional healing. I knew I needed to become whole within myself before I could gain ground. With each step, I was breaking a generational mindset.

I knew I didn't want a small life. I knew I was meant for something more.

I started off focusing on getting an education. My thought was that help me to get the jobs, be accepted in the boardroom and be able to break through. Once I'd graduated in my late thirties along with a pile of debt, I realized that wasn't the case. I'd thought with an education, hard work, and persistence that the success and money would follow. Nope!

I realise now I undervalued relationships. I didn't think I needed to dive into them and make them a priority. Why would I? If I had the education, the hard work and the work performance, I naturally would continue to climb the corporate ladder and make money. Instead, I was laid off. Not because of performance but because I didn't value creating lasting relationships with people.

A readjustment

So I knew I needed to do something different. I started my path by reaching out to business coaches and searching for clarity within my journey. I was not going to allow for an error in judgement and lack of value in relationships to prevent me from gaining success. I just had to readjust. And who in this life, doesn't occasionally have to readjust?

My pivot allowed me to take stock of the steps I had taken early on. Also, it allowed me to take a deeper dive into the reasons I wanted to be more. I just knew I was meant for more.

With my background, I had very strong skills in resourcefulness, persistence and grit. I was forward-thinking and willing to learn. I knew the path I was on was not one I wanted to stay on. I knew I had to seek out someone whose path I liked the look of. I needed to surround myself with like-minded individuals as doing so would provide the support for the life I was reaching for. The life that gave me freedom. Do not underestimate the power of surrounding yourself with people driving towards breaking through limiting generational beliefs.

I had an interesting upbringing. I grew up in a small town in the country with a Creek that I swam in almost daily. We lived in the same house my mom was born in. It was run down, but provided a space for my parents to raise children and survive. When I look back, I can see they did the best they could, but it was rough. We barely had food. If it weren't for our garden and my mom's ability to preserve, we would have gone without. They were surviving. They were raising a blended family of eight kids.

As I was the youngest, many of siblings were moving out when I was eight. Each following a path of generational poverty of which they didn't realize. Many of them went down the path of substance abuse and barely maintained a job, much less a career. It was hard to witness, but made me very clear about the life I didn't want. Moving to a path of success and wealth was a path not taken by my immediate family. My father, whom I loved very much, battled with his own demons. He went from a strong man filled with adventure in his heart to a man who was crippled by a back injury.

This caused a huge shift in the family dynamics. Mom, who wasn't a skilled trade worker, had to re-enter the workforce to support a family of 10. This caused increased anxiety - especially for my dad, who was riddled with depression. But through his pain in despair, he taught himself to become a locksmith. This allowed him to push through his depression and support his family. It gave him a purpose.

The shift

I realized in my late thirties that I also exhibited anxiety and depression. I too struggled, but for different reasons. I wanted so much more that I was blinded to all around me. I have traveled, I have explored, I have experienced amazing things and yet I when I lost my job, I lost a part of me. I lost my identity and I lost myself. Then, one day, I asked myself, *"why am I allowing my worth to be defined by a job?"* I knew I wasn't the only one to think this way. I knew others felt the crushing pain of unworthiness because they had lost their job, which they tied to their identity. I knew this was where I could help change not only my own mindset but help others find themselves again.

This experience is difficult enough but when mixed with a lack of support, the process can be prolonged. I too have experienced my significant other pulling me deeper into despair. This was a subtle shift - not respecting my boundaries, saying insulting things about my appearance and even suggesting that I was the reason for not getting hired right away - and I knew I had to make a big change. I had to make gains and standing still was not going to get me there.

This allowed me to seek coaches, get their advice and to execute it. As I was doing this, something rang true. I lived with a lie I'd told myself over and over again: you are what you came from; poor and unsuccessful. That a "real" life was one filled with money struggles. I sat there thinking, how and why did I live my life with such limiting beliefs? I couldn't stand still any longer and when I woke up with courage in my heart and DID IT, I found myself and my calling.

How did I get on this journey?

I had worked hard within the company I worked in. I continued to lean into my education in preparation for the promotion I was bound to achieve. I had worked through the ranks and plateaued at middle management. No longer was I climbing the ladder. I was stuck. I was ranked among my peers and within the company as the top 10%, but here I sat with a pile of debt and no promotion.

Fast forward 10 years and I was getting laid off. I didn't value relationships and focused on numbers, performing well, and hard work. With the fog of depression creeping in,

I knew this wasn't the life I wanted. It wasn't something I wanted to continue with. I had to make some changes fast. At the time this happened, I couldn't understand why I lost my job. Why things had happened the way they did. I know now that I was meant for something more. I was settling and things happened the way they did because complacency became my operating force. I was miserable. I was getting sick every month. I had severe ear infections, a busted ear drum and continued bouts of sickness. How can one live this way? Looking back, getting laid off was one of the best things to happen to me. The universe, GOD, knew I was meant for something more than what I was settling for. Sometimes the waves of change bring the best rewards.

During my quest for knowledge and something different, I took time to look within. Why did I think this way? Why did I believe that an education and hard work would automatically provide wealth? It was then that I realized I was raised with a belief system that didn't serve growth. It didn't provide a foundation of building a life above mine as a poor lower class family.

I made a quick pivot out of necessity. I started my own business helping others shed the belief systems that no longer served them and raise their energy to what they truly could be. I had to tear every part of their limiting beliefs down. I had to ask each of them, *"WHO SAYS SO? Why did this have to be? Why couldn't you be that person? Why couldn't you experience the wealth others experienced?"* The truth is, we all can. We just have to keep our mindset focused. We have to forego limited generational belief systems that no longer serve us.

Major challenge.

A major challenge is not finding what you want to present to the world, but gaining the right client, touching the right person and all of that at the right time.

While doing this work with others, I had to ensure my own mindset didn't fall back to old comfortable habits. You see, for me, when things get hard, it was easy to listen to that inner voice filled with negativity. It was easy to hear, "you're never going to make it!!" I had to tell it to leave. That this was not me and I would not fall back into the generational habits my family had been stuck in.

Each time you venture down the path of comfort, the path of familiar and un-serving, you must course correct. Each and every time!! This gets easier with more practice but can cause some relationships in your life to fall apart - cause people to pull you back into the comfortable; back into the familiar. This most often is by those closest to you. You are disrupting their comfortable place. Have you ever worked with a group of people who only wanted to do the bare minimum and you wanted a promotion? Did you witness how you were treated when you disrupted that bare minimum mindset? Did you see how they would ask you why? *"Why are you trying to make us look bad? Why do you want more?"* Then when you you continued on course, how they separated from you? This will happen. Be brave in your pursuit of your dream life. Be courageous in your pursuit of the person you deserve to be.

When this occurs, please keep focused. Keep the course. The reward is so worth it. To live in peace of mind in the life you created for yourself. Working with freedom from a corporation that valued you only as a number and used your genius for their gain. Above all, remember, you can't have gains by standing still.

Break through

Each and every internal battle I had with myself made me stronger. It allowed me to discredit each and every negative thought, because I was meant for more. YOU ARE MEANT FOR MORE TOO! This life does not have to be lived in doubt, poverty and a generational mindset that no longer serves you.

In my life, with failed relationships and unemployment, I knew that my belief systems no longer served me and I couldn't stand still and make gains. I had to break through! I had to shut off the noise and recognize that the woman who had pushed through the bullsh*t of her own limited generational beliefs can help others do the same.

When I found my inner power I recognized how I can support those around me. Pushing for better within myself allowed for me to assist others do the same. This life gave me freedom to provide clarity around what is holding one back.

The steps

The following steps took me some time to get into and to teach myself. It is not easy, but if you dare to do the work you will find yourself breaking through. It will be ugly and you will realise many types of emotions. This is normal and encouraged. When you often feel the most resistance is when you are on the verge of soaring. DON'T STOP!

1. Look within and ask yourself, what lies do you tell yourself? What does that inner voice say when no one else is listening?

2. Ask yourself, do those beliefs serve YOU? Do they make you who you are? Do they limit your gains? Do they stop you being YOU?

3. Make small promises to yourself and keep them. Mine was getting up in the morning and showering daily. This helped me set the stage for a growth mindset.

4. Write down how you want to see yourself. Get very specific. What will you look like? What is your typical day? How will you feel? What do you drive? What do you live in? How are your relationships?

5. THEN LIVE THAT WAY! The mind will follow and seek what you think of. If you think of what and how to achieve the things you see yourself as, you WILL SUCCEED. Seek a coach. Business coaches are a necessity. They allow you to gain guidance on their success.

These steps are best served with hard work. You only can shift that generational mindset by doing, failing and doing again. You have to get really honest with yourself. You have to tear apart each and every thought. You have to turn away from situations, from people, from others that no longer serve you. You have to move along the path of a life that you deserve and want more than the air you breathe. Turning away from situations that are comfortable for the unknown is scary. But don't shy away from the fear. Embrace it! Acknowledge it! Keep gaining! Keep moving!

Breaking through generational limiting beliefs is freeing. I remember being held down by all the limiting beliefs I held onto. I remember how hopeless at times I felt. I still have days where I have to remind myself to keep moving. You see, all of us are meant to live happy fulfilling lives. We are destined to have a life filled with experiences that reach beyond our comfort zone. Who says you must settle for less? Settle for a life filled with struggle? Break through the limiting beliefs that no longer serve you and feel free. Don't limit yourself.

Generational mindsets are hard to push aside. There will be times you may want to quit. There will be times you question the path you are walking. The path you are traveling down. Know that to feel success often means aligning what you were meant for. This is discovered by doing. You will make mistakes. There will be times you want to quit. There will be times you say to yourself, *"this isn't the path."* In those moments it's important to take stock of the *why. Why* are you feeling this way? Is it fear? Is it your generational mindset? This is very important as you don't want to stop once you start. It is important to note that when you feel this way, it is normal. It is okay. You will just want to feel it, acknowledge it and break through it.

When you start, do it messily. Do it boldly. Do it authentically. Sometimes the doing isn't the final resting spot, but one that you need to keep moving. Do not stand still. These beliefs are subtle and are hardwired in our upbringing and we continue to validate them with our stories. STOP THAT! You truly can be what you are brave enough to be. You can break through. At the end of the day, you can't have gains by standing still. Create, do and live the life you WANT.

You are the only thing holding yourself back.

I know I was.

About the author

Sabrina Cochran grew up in a small town in a blended family. She pushed beyond generational poverty and quickly pivoted to what has now become her purpose. Helping others overcome limiting generational beliefs that no longer serve them. She had a break though herself, which is why this work is her passion.

Facebook: Sabrina Rae

Email: Sabrina.R.Cochran@gmail.com

Shan Simpson

How it started

As another year starts, many will make promises, as they always do, to have the results they never achieved in previous years, because they didn't embody the change to make them happen.

That wasn't going to happen this particular year to me. I had had enough. My words and intentions now needed to have substance and purpose - they needed action. I needed to create my breakthrough. I knew if I left it another year - only speaking of what was to be and what was to be let go of - I would have reinforced my spiralling self belief, which was something that others had created. It wasn't my truth but was the reality I was living. The reality I had allowed. The potential I knew I had was deep down within me.

Have you been in that position? Have you felt that moment

where you know you are worth more, but felt trapped by your environment, relationships or finances? Where you realised your belief in you, in what was possible, had been eroded and influenced by others who never valued you in the first place?

Well, if this is you, I know how you feel. Because that was me a few short years ago. But I learnt that to have the best, you must become your best.

Was it scary? The unknown? The uncharted water? Most definitely. But it was scarier to stay where I was.

Of course, I was afraid of taking those first steps but what I can tell you now is that this fear is temporary. When I identified and accepted what made my life miserable, the choice became simple: either stay as I was or face my fear, knowing one would potentially give me the breakthrough I so desperately needed, while the other would keep me exactly where I was and didn't want to be.

So I chose the fear.

I embarked on seeking out those who were non judgemental and empowering; those who had the tools that would equip and educate me to not only save myself but to enable me to help others who were in the same situation. Who were fearful of taking their first step. For it is one thing to free yourself of the invisible chains, but to free others as well, so that they may fly to their new heights, to live their truth and not the reality of others… that was an empowerment I hadn't felt before but I knew I wanted.

I learnt quickly, I had to raise my self worth, I had to start acting the way that I wanted to be seen, even before my reality had caught up. This allowed me to associate with those who I needed to surround myself with, who helped to lift, nurture and grow me into what I wanted to become.

This association helped me to walk through new door and, more importantly, made it easier to close the old doors that never served me, but had kept me suspended, motionless, in a life that had no purpose.

My journey

My insight into business started at the age of 11 as my parents owned and ran a bar.

It was here that I experienced my real first taste of

entrepreneurship. Yet in my early adulthood, I found myself moving further away from a business ownership mindset to a herd mindset. Reflecting back now, that's where I sensed the fences of conformity were closing in on me

I found myself in a career path for a decade with British Airways. I got used to being told what I had to do, where I had to be and how long I had to do it for. Yes, I got to travel to the destinations I'd only dreamed of but I never got to enjoy them when I got there - it was always such a quick turnaround. But it did give me fuel to know that travel was a passion. Over time, that vision of entrepreneurship from my early childhood resurfacing and I knew my current career path wasn't for me. I knew I needed to start making major changes.

My true epiphany was that entrepreneurship was my passion, though I'd only ever dabbled - never taking it too seriously - as I knew I had an income.

I decided to go all in with my business. It was now time to take it seriously and I had to make the decision to move from being a hobbyist to becoming a professional entrepreneur. I realised that my daily habits had to change drastically .

I needed to take massive action. I had to create new connections from networking at business events, learn how to communicate and position my offering, to be of greater value in order to stand out from others in the market.

There was so much I had to learn and I didn't have the luxury to wait until I was ready. I had to learn on the job. I no longer had the safety net of an income outside of what I was now creating.

I learned quickly that the key was to remove idle distractions in order to better focus on the things that would generate the most income. The first goal was simple: that within a year I had to earn the several thousands I'd invested into the business and my learning back.

It became a success and I quickly created a multiple 6 figure business. But there was something missing. My passion was travel, yet my travel business had started to own me. I found myself sending people where they wanted to go, being at their beck and call, all the while, they were not being able to enjoy the luxurious vacations I had created for them. I realised that I was creating something for others that I wasn't participating in and I didn't like it.

Here was my second *"Ah ha!"* moment. I wanted to create some form of ongoing passive income that would allow me to participate in what I had created.

I read a book that exposed me to the concept of building a business that you could remove yourself from and still watch the income streaming in. A business that allowed you to enjoy the fruits of your labour.

This now was my greatest shift - not just to own a business, but to own a business that didn't own me. I had to look for a way that could fulfill the time equation.

You see, there are many that have all the time, yet they don't have the money. There are many, they have all the money, but don't have the time. The masses, unfortunately, don't have enough of either and yet are the busiest. Only a few have learnt to create an income stream that allows them the time to enjoy and participate in the lifestyle their work has created for others.

My driving factor now became all about helping others to create a life they could actually participate because they'd found a way to generate income in their absence.

The new business needed to be something that would serve others, bring true value and provide solutions to a real need. I quickly broke that down into two areas: health and finances.

Lack of both of these causes great anxiety globally. I knew I could get behind the idea of improving the lives of entrepreneurs by improving their health and wellness, as well as helping them to establish their financial prosperity.

For me, this was a totally different arena from the travel one that I had known. It's important to understand that even though I knew I had to change, I wasn't looking in this direction initially. Sometimes, our solutions are not going to be found where we're searching.

Now, here was the bridge that I had to cross. I had gone out and shared my passion for travel and invested tens of thousands into that business. How was I now going to approach people with a new message ? What were others going to think?

I had to learn to pivot. Luckily, there was one thing at the core of both ventures: my personal passion to serve and impact others.

Once again, I found myself in the position of having to learn something I knew nothing about. This time, though, that excited me. Gaining new knowledge felt empowering as I knew it would enable me to pay forward my own good fortune; to see hope in the eyes of others with their health and to see their financial situations improving.

The biggest lesson here for me was to be open to learning something new. Because it's in those uncharted waters that the greatest experiences can be gained. I recalled the fear of stepping out in the very beginning, but this time I knew that fear was only temporary and I was able to turn it into excitement - excitement about the new chapter, excitement about the possibilities and excitement of making a difference on a significant level.

I was used to booking destinations and now I was learning as fast as I possibly could about selling health products. One, was a destination that you could see, the other wasn't - it was helping others to improve their health on a cellular level - something they couldn't see - and that was a major shift.

But when you can remove the doubt of what one is consuming and validate it independently, you have a genuine opportunity to make the world a healthier place -

and that was certainly worth getting passionate and purposeful about.

Within a few short months, my personal journey experienced a significant improvement, and I knew it was time to release my grip on my travel business so I could embrace my new venture with both hands.

I was reminded once again that you can't grab the future with both hands if you're holding onto the past with one. So many times we want security - we want greater things in our lives - but we aren't willing to take a risk and step away from the very things that we want to change.

Today, the world is the unhealthiest it has ever been, yet we have access to more information than at any other time in mankind's history. Many are experiencing anxiety about their financial wellbeing, even though we are all surrounded by so many opportunities. It didn't make sense to me. Something was missing.

Crossing the bridge

It takes courage to let go of what we know and to embrace the unknown. It has to come from a desire for more as that's the only thing that will drive you over the bridge we all must cross.

This bridge is in everyone's lives. Across it is everything that we desire. Learning to cross it isn't easy and we will most certainly need to do things that we do not want to do. But that is what separates those who have from those who have not. It's nothing to do with talent or capability. It's all to do with overcoming your fear, leaving your comfort zone and crossing that bridge.

Many have lived in a coma of complacency for too long, having lost sight of what once had emotionally moved them. They lack clarity, having not identified what's important to them and are living life passively rather than a life they have created by design.

You need to find a community that you align with; a message of legitimate value and purpose that moves you, that wakes you, that stirs you. When you do that, you will never look at the effort or the inconveniences, you'll only look at it as a journey that's moving you towards the destination of your hopes and desires.

The greatest reward is who you will become on the journey.

This is the pride of your endeavours. You can have everything you desire if you make that decision to take these first steps. Greatness is inside everyone and awaits those willing to face their fears. Those willing to cross that bridge.

The steps

1. Actions speak louder than words

As I've said, that bridge is in every one of our lives. I know now what is possible, for I have started to cross that bridge myself. The key for me was the daily disciplines I implemented: accountability and actionable, measurable goals that were implemented in a timely manner. These are just some of the things I had to learn and master. We all know that words are empty unless action is applied to them each day.

2. Prioritise

I start each day with gratitude. I remind myself of my purpose which gives me clarity of vision and has taught me to prioritise the things that will move me towards the goals I set, not get distracted by things that will just keep me busy, because it's the right actions that make the progress. There's a significance between activity and accomplishment - the former is just being busy whilst the latter is getting the job done.

3. Be consistent

You see too many talented people never reach their potential because they never apply what they know consistently. When you master your daily disciplines and you embrace the consistency of activity, then it's possible to surpass those with more talent.

4. Go the extra mile

Success is a planned event, so my daily activities are what drives me. These include having new conversations, making new connections and honouring my word. Most importantly, it's following through, as this is here where success happens. You have to go the extra mile because it's never crowded. In my experience, there are no extraordinary people, there are only ordinary people who do a little extra.

My purpose now is to raise faith-filled female leaders, who can not only impact those around them today, but generations to follow.

Today I'm a successful entrepreneur. I'm very proud of my achievements, but it is only the beginning. I've opened myself up to a life full of possibilities and also been willing to face risk, failure and vulnerability. This has been the true test of what I declared to be important to me and is the thing that allowed me to end the year differently to the one before.

I made the decision to let the tongue in my shoes speak louder than the tongue in my mouth.

I wanted not just a life of choices, but the time to enjoy those choices I'd created for myself and my sons.Today I am well on the way to a life of design.

Dreams are to be chased, but along the way, fears are to be faced. Goals are there to help you grow and you shouldn't be afraid of setting them - there's nothing that's unattainable if you go after it, if you're willing to grow through it, if you're willing to pay a price for it.

Go strongly forward in the direction of your hopes, desires and dreams, because they are waiting for you to own them. Now go do the work for them.

I believe in you.

About the Author

Shantarl is a high energy, inspiring motivational speaker and business owner. Shan's seen the highs and lows of the entrepreneurial life cycle with her various successes in the 'home based business' market and she knows what it takes to be a full time mum and working from home .

Shantarl's passion is to inspire all women - whether you're a mum or not - to prove that they can "have it all" by showing them how she has done it and how to achieve it for themselves. This is a woman who loves to see others shine brighter than they ever thought possible. She believes in YOU!

Website: www.shantarl.com
Facebook: www.Facebook.com/shantarl
Email: hello@shantarl.com

Sonia Ovenden

How it started

I'd just finished my photo shoot and had to pinch myself. OMG, I'd made it. Being featured in Forbes was only ever a dream, but now I'd selected the picture to accompany my story. Me, a girl from the West Midlands, UK, had made it.

Just three years prior I'd had a health scare and I put four months of my life on hold, unsure whether or not I had breast cancer. I created a bucket list, which was fun. But then I flipped the question, what would happen if I was okay?

My husband is the man of my dreams and I had a very successful career, drawing a salary many people could only ever dream of. I loved the people I worked with and they respected me for the role I did. I travelled to amazing countries with my job. Japan, China, Rwanda, Egypt, Hong Kong - the list went on. Yet each morning, I could feel that something was missing and it exhausted me all the time. I was too tired to enjoy the money, my marriage and the lifestyle right on my doorstep in Dubai. I should have been happy, but was existing rather than living.

By everyone else's standards I'd made it, yet in my heart I knew things had to change. In some ways, I guess I was living the life mapped out for me since the day I was born: study, get a job, build a career, buy a home and get married, but I knew I wanted more from life. I just wasn't sure what and was afraid I'd never find it - whatever *"it"* was.

When I quit my corporate job, my fears were incredible. What was I *doing*? My hands were shaking as I said goodbye to my amazing CEO, wonderful Director and colleagues.

As I scan my Forbes article, I feel proud that I kept going, though sometimes I nearly didn't. There are days I still can't believe I found the courage to walk away from the familiar, though I know I'm grateful I did. On occasions, I'd say to my husband, "I think I'll get a normal job", but as soon as the words left my mouth, I knew it wasn't what I wanted. One of my favourite quotes is from Henry Ford: *"If you think you can, or you think you can't, either way you're right."* And how true it is. I've lost count of the number of days where I was close to giving up on my dream, and ready to step back into the norm, or the number of times where my husband believed in me more than I ever believed in myself.

Alongside his belief, being clear on my *"why"* was instrumental in keeping me going. That, along with my determination and tenacity, helped. In the corporate world, building strong relationships was paramount and I focussed on developing and helping people. My coaching business would be no different. I knew in my head that it could work, that I'd done it working for others and there was no reason I couldn't do it for myself. Above all else, and even on my most doubting days, somewhere deep within, I knew I'd make it. I knew that whatever perceived obstacle or hurdle stood in front of me was there for a reason. I knew things would work out - that I could build my business to help others create a life they loved living.

Growing up, my parents taught me to work hard for a living and, on reflection, I took this to the extreme. I wanted to be the best I could be and never give people room to criticise me – I never enjoyed being told off.

Consequently, I excelled in every job I did, whether that was cleaning barge boats with Mum when I was thirteen for extra money or my bar job in a local bowling alley. Whenever I left a company, they wanted me to stay and I liked it that way.

Eventually, I fell into training and development, something that wasn't even a thing when I was considering a career. I worked my way up the corporate ladder and led an exceptional team. I thought I'd made it, but the excitement and drive which I'd assumed would come didn't appear. As I continued to work full time and with the support of my company, I studied for my postgraduate degree followed by my MSc. I never realised how impactful these two degrees would be, but almost every day now I express gratitude towards that company for all the opportunities they brought me: first, my husband and second, for sponsoring me in gaining the qualifications. My husband is one of the greatest gifts in my life and, with the help of my degrees, more doors were opened and I was able to secure a job overseas.

The financial rewards in this new role were huge but the hours were ridiculously long. Over time and across different geographies, I experienced burnt out - I realised I was still the same rat, just competing in a different race.

Fear of the unknown

When I finally found the courage to leave, it was the first step in building my coaching business, or so I thought. I guess the universe had other ideas by almost immediately testing me on how much I wanted it. Within a matter of weeks, a job back in the corporate world came up and I took it, albeit for all the wrong reasons. I thought the reasons to do it were great - to help a friend who needed my expertise and it was just three days a week - though now I realise I was just getting in my own way. On reflection, my subconscious fears were surfacing. I was afraid I wouldn't make it on my own and I didn't want to let anyone down. It took this experience for me to realise that helping others become the best version of themselves is what I love to do.

I had always tried to make time for self-development, though it was often as an afterthought following everyone else's. I ventured into a more structured journey of self-discovery and learnt so much more. I began to explore questions such as, why do we do the things we do? Or react the way we do? What beliefs and values do we have? Are they ours, or have we inherited them?

My journey was nothing short of life changing and, as I increased my consciousness in everyday life, I could see what I truly wanted in my life. I knew deep within me I should continue to help people and so for the second and final time, I walked away from the corporate world. Though I now have corporate clients, I can share my expertise from the outside for the highest good of all.

The overwhelming fears crept in - *"am I not good enough? Will I get clients? What if I fail?"* - but one day, as I sat at my desk typing the ending to my first novel, I felt an overwhelming sense of clarity. So what if I tried and it didn't work? At least I'd know I'd given it everything I had. And in that moment, I faced the fear, acknowledged it and took action. I instead focused on the idea of, *"what's the worst thing that could happen?"* It's now a habit and I continue to embrace every challenge for what it is: an opportunity for growth.

***

I didn't realise that deciding to start my business would in fact be the easiest and most straightforward part of the process.

I had so many rules about how things should look. My perfectionist persona was coming to the forefront. Perhaps it was all the rules and conditioning I'd picked up along the corporate journey. I needed a website, a logo, a brand, a message and was reading all these books describing the best way to build a business; about what you should and shouldn't do. But some books I was scouring had conflicting opinions. All this before the panic of actually getting clients set in. What services would I offer? How would they look? How can I charge people for helping them? What price should I charge? It was ridiculous; the internal self-chatter was deafening.

As I explored how I wanted to position myself as a life coach, the comparison trap was extreme. There are many experts spanning myriad of backgrounds that have a huge number of followers - how would there be room for little old me? There are so many coaches in the market, what makes my coaching unique? What's my USP?

Then came the logistics. Setting up a company, a licence to trade in a foreign country and a business bank account as an expat living overseas wasn't easy. I thought perhaps I was on the wrong path - surely, it wouldn't be this difficult if it was the right one? I kept wondering if I was being tested again or pushed to give up. Thankfully I never did, though some days I accomplished less than others.

Next, came the fear of getting clients. Putting myself out there was one of the biggest challenges of all. It was time to be seen but I was afraid of what people would think - that people would judge me, mock or even ridicule me.

I was wobbling and, if I'm honest, my self-doubt was off the charts. Giving up would have been the easiest choice but I knew from the depths of my soul that this was what I was meant to do. I couldn't turn back. And on the days where I came very close to giving up, I borrowed my husband's belief in me, which helped and gave me time to find my own again.

Overcoming

Over time, I realised I had everything I needed within me, just as I now coach and guide my clients to remember. In fact, turning to the tools I'd coached my clients with - that "do as I say" attitude - was what helped me begin to move forwards.

Fear had held me back too many times but as I realised that fear can only exist in the past and the future, I focussed more on the *now* and decided to do what I wanted anyway. I saw fear as my friend and worked through it each time it showed up. I'm not saying I'm no longer afraid of things, but I'm able to turn the fears I do have into a more positive experience.

When I was losing momentum, I took time out and focussed on my "why". Why had I started on this journey? What was driving me to do this? I found reconnecting with and remembering my "why" provided a new level of commitment. I also found setting intentions for the day of how I wanted to feel a great comfort through the flatter times.

Someone said the three most dangerous words in the English

language are, *"I know that."* I pondered this and saw the truth in the statement. Try it! Each time we say the words, what action step follows? If you are anything like me, very little - it's as if knowing is all that matters. I'm so grateful I stumbled upon this as soon as I did, and I could expand the statement to include, "and now what?"

My ability to build relationships throughout my life and career has carried me far and mattered when I was out of sorts. I'd never been good at asking for help, but discovered that doing so was what kept me going and connected. I recognised the transition I'd blindly navigated from "going" to work being surrounded by people to becoming a lone worker with me, myself and I. Soon enough I reached out for support and people to bounce ideas off, learning that just because I worked by myself, it didn't mean I had to be alone. These people are now some of my biggest cheerleaders and believers - like a personal fan base.

I faced many challenges - as I know many of you have or will - and my level of optimism proved invaluable. The internal compass to feel what the good could be in any challenge enabled me to keep going and not get swamped by doubt and fear. Optimism is a must, and should we choose it, is something we can develop. When things happened TO me, I would spiral down a mental path of doom and gloom, which I'm sure many of us can relate to. But what happens if we change just one two-letter word? What happens when we say "when things happen FOR me" instead? I interrupted my own thoughts and asked this time and time again, when all I could originally see was things happening *to* me. In choosing the perspective from which I come, I can see the opportunities in front of me. And so can you.

The steps

1. Be clear on your *"why"*

Whether you're just starting out, or facing uncertainty and challenges, remembering your *"why"* is crucial. Journal around your *why*, asking questions of yourself as you go. For example, why did you embark on this journey? What is it you want to achieve? Is what you're doing/creating what you'd love to do? The closer we get to understanding and feeling into our *"why"* the more we can navigate the journey in the comfort of everything being aligned. Sometimes, we may need to change our course a little to stay on track and, in doing so, we bring a revived level of determination and tenacity.

2. Set Intentions

At the start of each day, ask, how do I want to feel today? What positive and empowering emotions do I want to experience throughout the day? Identify five each morning and write them down. Before you go to bed, review the list and see just how many you experienced and I know it will amaze you how many you felt. The power of setting pure intentions is incredible.

3. Take Action

Are you reading this chapter and saying, *"I know that"*? Remember, these three words often stop us from taking action. We never grow out of needing to know things, but for many it stops there. I'm here to say: *and now what*? What action step can you take today which will move you closer to your goal or dream? No matter how small, 1% each day is progress. Imagine you want to write a novel and if we took an average of a seventy-five thousand word-count, it would mean writing just 750 words to achieve 1% progress - far more achievable than looking at the entire book. When we take a step back from the whole, there is always one step we can take right where we are. What action step can you take today?

4. Choose Your Cheerleaders

Take time out to identify and recognise those people who will support, encourage and help you on your journey. As we grow and become the people we aspire to be, some of our existing relationships may fall away. And yes, this can feel uncomfortable. When change occurs, our resistance to the change is what can slow things down, including people moving out of our circle to make way for those who will enhance our journey. Look around you. Who can you call on for help? Which people can be your cheerleaders to lift you when needed? Who believes in you so much that when your own self-belief dwindles, you can borrow theirs for a while? Commit to contact those who you believe will be your biggest cheerleader and ask if they will take on the role. What will you need from them?

5. Embrace the Fear & Choose the Perspective

We've explored how fear can stop us in our tracks, so stand up to them. Identify your top three fears right now. Is there a theme emerging? Gain clarity around your fears. Are you afraid of what might happen? Are you afraid of history repeating itself? Right here, right now, does the fear exist? Is your fear presenting an opportunity for growth? With each fear you identified, ask yourself, *"why is this happening FOR me?"* What if the opposite were true?

Often, we fear failure itself, or so we think. But if we keep asking ourselves the question *"why"* it can lead to different discoveries. For example, if I succeed, I'm afraid some of my friends won't like it - the fear is the opposite of failure and links to the fear of losing someone through success. As we learn to pattern-interrupt our thoughts and bring awareness to them, the growth and progress is far better than we ever could have imagined. As a fear creeps in, stop and ask yourself, *"one, two, three, why is this happening FOR me?"* and then consider how you can reframe the three fears you've identified to bring about empowered action.

***

I know you'll have done plenty of research into the best ways to build or grow your business. And I also know that fear of the *"what ifs"* and *"I'm not good enough"* will creep in along the way - and it's okay to wobble. Be kind with yourself and celebrate even the smallest of wins. Remember, learning takes time and we are all a work in progress. Just know that you are bigger than any obstacle you face and you can make this happen - there is only one of you and the world needs what you have to offer!

About the Author

As a certified Life Mastery Consultant, Sonia can help you design and manifest a life you love living.

Sonia has worked with a variety of clients including CEO's, entrepreneurs, professionals and other coaches, helping them build their dreams, accelerate their results and create richer, more fulfilling lives.

She has featured on Forbes, appeared on UK Radio and mentors others in their quest to become a coach. She has written her debut novel and is currently in the early stages of her second.

As a certified Love and Authenticity, and Whole Healing Practitioner with an MSc in Human Resource Development and a professional journey steeped in learning and personal growth, she continues to inspire people across the world to new heights of success, meaning and aliveness.

For over 25 years Sonia has been studying and implementing transformational success principles, and as a sought-after trainer, author and certified life coach, Sonia's workshops and coaching programs help people break through limitations and achieve greater results than they've known before.

If you are looking to increase your clarity, amplify your confidence, and achieve your next level of success, while enjoying the highest levels of fulfilment in life, Sonia's coaching programs can help you get there.

Website: www.discoverthebeautyofyou.com
Facebook: www.facebook.com/discoverthebeautyofyou
www.facebook.com/sonia.biddle.5/
Email: sonia@discoverthebeautyofyou.com

Stephanie Bourbon

How it started

I'm a writer, then…there's everything else. I never wanted to be an entrepreneur or work freelance, but here I am after twenty years of doing it and BOOM, I now own my own company. I always wanted to do something I loved and I refused to settle for a dull "day job" to pay the bills. I mean, you can't take money with you, so having a job that is just that - a job to make money - wasn't ever something I would accept for myself. Life is too short not to be happy.

Let's back up. To understand where I am and how I got here, you need to know how it started. I was an actress - that's how my creative life began - and not the famous kind. I was the waitress waiting tables by day and night and auditioning in between shifts. When I was in New York, I was a nanny for a bit, so I had a roof overhead while auditioning and studying my craft. One day I went to an audition for a voice part in a Disney film; I knew I wouldn't get it, but it was

Disney, so I thought it would be fun. In the middle of a song, the director stopped me and asked if I ever wanted to be in animation. I was deeply offended. "I'm an actress!". He showed me the doodles I had done on the call sheet while waiting for my turn and said, "you are an artist." I replied something sarcastic about how I was just bored and scribbling people in the waiting room, then went home called my mother and complained about the nerve of Disney. Cut to four years later, and I worked in feature animation as an artist. Then, September 11ᵗʰ happened, and everyone slashed jobs, so I picked up freelance work here and there. I started writing the great American romantic comedy before it was a thing.

I pitched movies while working at Disney as I had always wanted to write. I'm a born storyteller; it's just who I am. As a child, my dream was to become a famous actress and then write and star in my own films. I mean, *Rocky* did it, so why couldn't I? Maybe that's what comes of watching too many movies as a kid or growing up on the East Coast where *Rocky* was HUGE. I saw *Star Wars* and immediately fell in love with Luke Skywalker and storytelling. I was a kid, but I was still blown away by the story. Then I read *The Shining* and knew that storytelling would be a massive part of my life and that I would write. I had some detours; that's okay. It all got me here, coaching female writers and helping them reach their goals.

Now, when animation crashed, I had nothing. I was so broke that I couldn't even eat every day, it was terrible and, what was worse, there were thousands of us all in the same boat. Before social media, we met at Starbucks and complained or emailed around or had actual phone calls about how hard it was. And it was hard. The thing is that since animation was booming to the public and it was only traditional or hand-drawn animation that had disappeared overnight, it was hard for people on the outside to understand what it was really like out here in Los Angeles. While working here and there on freelance art jobs in animation, I wrote a couple of novels. I looked at boring jobs but, honestly, I wasn't qualified to do them. Going to college for musical theatre and working pretty much only as an actress, an artist in a particular niche of animation and being good at creative writing didn't exactly make me a fit for even jobs that anyone could do. It was demoralizing, to say the least and I felt like a failure.

I even moved up to Seattle to try to work in PR, which I was good at, but they were also cutting jobs left, right, and center, so I returned to Los Angeles, realizing that I couldn't survive in the real world. Most people leave Los Angeles because they can't cut it in the entertainment industry, but I couldn't make it outside of this industry. I went back to feature animation in Burbank in the spring of 2003 for a couple of months. The last day I was at Disney (they were cutting those who had managed to stay through the initial crash) I was like, *"yeah, I've been out of steady work for two years, so it's no biggie,"* which was something I was grateful for and yet I was terrified. I filed bankruptcy two months later and ended up on the floor crying because I had hit rock bottom. In my 30s, was college-educated, worked for Disney, had films optioned as a writer... and yet I was unemployed. I decided to get my first humorous novel published. That was another debacle, but I was a survivor and I knew that I would be okay. I was scrappy.

My new life had emerged, and I was a sole proprietor working as a freelance artist and once the novel was out, I started getting offers to write as a ghostwriter. I did that for a long time on a top-rated book series, but I never got the credit. At the time, I didn't care because I wanted the money and I wanted to work as a creative. Determination and being scrappy at networking and finding paying gigs became my forte because I was good at it. Sure - on paper, it looked like I was failing, but I wasn't; I was succeeding, though I couldn't see it at the time.

I made it happen because I didn't have a choice but was also dealing with something that would change my path forever. My mother, also an artist but way more practical than I am, was dying and it was crushing my soul. I was out in California taking every job I could find and living some weeks with no money and others with a lot but never having enough to save and I couldn't even visit her because she was in Arizona. It was devastating. She died in 2004 and I took a job on a film in Denmark as an artist. Essentially, I ran away. I had to. I was also rewriting the novel - the one I mentioned before. I put everything I had into my writing and the animation job in Copenhagen was good, but I knew that it wouldn't last, so I started thinking about how I would survive when it ended.

Oddly enough, another animation job came up, so I took it. It was in Arizona, the state my mom lived and died. It was tough emotionally, but I finished the rewrites on the novel while having some financial security (or so I thought) and because my life is God's favorite sitcom, that ended in five months instead of five years. I was out of work again, but my new novel was about to come out, so I thought it would be okay because, in my head, I'd be rich. Of course, that didn't happen.

Rock bottom

I came back to Los Angeles and, again, my being scrappy helped me stay afloat. I took jobs as a personal assistant, writer's assistant and working-for-hire as a writer here and there between animation gigs. After all those years, I realized that I worked for myself, but I didn't have my own company officially. I was a contract worker. I was still very depressed over my mother's death when my father had a massive heart attack and ended up on life support. That turned into six years of him living in a home with dementia. I was once again drowning. Staying afloat became all I could do.

Then, someone offered me a job on a TV show as a writer after seeing me on MySpace trying to be funny about how bad things were. He was a producer and was like, *"Hey, I read your book; ever thought about writing for television?"* I had already written a pilot TV show, a screenplay, and worked in the industry, so I was like, *"YES!"* I took that job on a show which was canceled before I even got one-episode credit. Once again, I was down and out, but I was optimistic because it's who I am. I took courses in TV writing to learn everything about the business. I also applied for every fellowship and writing program the studios had to offer. I was pushing 40, but I didn't care or believe that age would be an issue; it was. Still, I wrote a terribly formatted spec script of a show for a fellowship and they liked my storytelling and voice so much I was offered a job full stop, but then the WGA strike happened and, just like that, I was out of work, again. This went on for three years. I applied for things that didn't work out. I took freelance animation and started illustrating children's books to cover the bills. I kept writing everything. Failure was not an option.

The breakthrough

In 2006, I joined a challenge to write a novel in a month. I was unemployed and it kept my mind off of things. I finished that novel and it was published in 2007 by a small publishing house, which was a huge confidence builder for me, but I was still not working or bringing in an income. I decided to start consulting wannabe TV writers. I charged them what I needed to cover my bills. I gave them specific advice on what classes they needed for their particular writing goals. I helped them have better success in their genre and where they wanted to be. You probably have no idea how complex television writing can be. It matters if the show is on cable or network, or there is cursing, or drinking, or crime, or maybe it's a comedy, and then is there a single camera or a multi-camera, and those need to be formatted differently! It's so confusing and you can spend years in the wrong courses. I created a *concierge service* for writers to help them and help me pay the rent.

Then, in 2010, the first significant shift happened for me. I was broke, broke, broke. My mom was dead; my father was in a home. I was 41, single, and had no way to pay rent. I had no idea what I would do. Despite all my scrappiness, there were no animation jobs and I had nothing. I think that I had about ten dollars to my name - I'm not even exaggerating. The situation was dire, and I needed money, so here is what I did. I posted on Facebook something like, *"does anyone want to learn dialogue? I'm good at it, so I'm going to have an online course starting in two weeks, and it's $350. Send me a message or PayPal me at this email."* And just like that, I had an online course. Ten people signed up in less than three hours, and I had enough to pay rent. I hadn't planned on doing this, so I scrambled to come up with a course on the fly. Every Sunday, I'd create lessons and email them out. I knew nothing about how to run an online course. I had taken many writing courses via Zoom-type software or email, so that's what I did. It was the easiest $3500 I had ever made.

I was back on top! YAY! It didn't last financially; I decided to start pitching around a book on dialogue and even though it didn't sell, I started getting invited to give talks on it. People began contacting me to do consulting work. I was already an entrepreneur, but my mindset wasn't there. *Until it was.*

I had reached a breakthrough with the dialogue course and even though I was broke and having rejections on the book, I kept pivoting and sending out other ideas. I took on more and more writing clients while pitching screenplays, working as a reader for the studios and, of course, as an artist. In my mind, I was a creative coach as well as an artist and a writer. Now I have my own creative consulting business, I still draw and I'm a writer. I can't imagine not doing any of them.

The things that got me here were all over the place. Still, the steps that I took to be successful were a combination of the following: being scrappy, pivoting, keeping a positive attitude in the face of rejection and rewriting my own story.

Being a creative for a living isn't easy. It's hard financially and emotionally and it's a lot like being an entrepreneur. You have to be able to take rejection and learn from it. During these years, I kept repeating to myself, *"if you don't like something change it and if you can't change it, change your mindset."* That quote helped me always find a way. The things I did throughout the last twenty years were mostly around networking and staying in touch with people. I find that being positive instead of negative helped a lot. If I sent an email or posted that I was broke and desperate, nothing would come, but if I turned it into, *"I'm free and looking for my next thing"* jobs and money would come to me. In 2014 I decided to take business classes and learn how to do online courses properly. I admit that at that time, I was only working one on one with writers as I wrote and worked as an artist. In 2019 I officially opened my new company, Judanie Bean Creative Consulting, and it's growing steadily as I add more courses and pivot as I need to. 2020 was devastating for so many, but it's allowed me to reach many writers who otherwise wouldn't consider online learning. I was building my authority around being able to go to writing conferences and network at screenwriting and TV writing events around town. All that changed, and so I pivoted again. I'm the queen of the pivot.

The steps

Being able to shift my mindset and plans quickly has helped me go from staying afloat to swimming swiftly. Rejection will come - especially to anyone who has a job based on the opinion of talent, such as writers, artists, actresses/actors, dancers, singers and musicians. To do well in a creative industry, one has to take rejection, learn from it and cast it aside.

Here are some steps that I take that have changed my mindset from one of despairing and broke to one of hope and prosperity.

Step 1

Take in the rejection and reflect on it. Learn from it. Shift your mindset from *"I suck"* to, *"this is how I can improve,"* - whatever it is.

Step 2

Always look for other opportunities. When one door closes, another opens and every no is a step closer to a yes. Don't fixate on the nos, but focus on what you could do now because that thing you wanted didn't happen.

Step 3

Manage your expectations and goals to something realistic and attainable. If your goal is to hit the New York Times Best Seller List, but you don't have an agent for your work, you are setting yourself up for failure, disappointment, and heartbreak. Your goal could be to finish your project and find a new agent because that is attainable from where you are now.

Step 4

Practice gratitude with everything. Sure, it's okay to vent, but then move on. I have a gratitude journal that I write three things that I'm grateful for every morning and that sets the tone for the whole day.

Step 5

Believe you can do it and know your worth. It's easy to get discouraged, but you can shift your belief system by writing things down. I am great. "I am worth it. I am enough. I am powerful. I am successful." Whatever it is that speaks to you. Also, honestly, meditating on this helps too.

When I was sixteen, I saw *Back to the Future* and it taught me that if I put my mind to it, I could do anything. I believe that. My advice is to go after your dreams, don't settle for less than and be willing to pivot when you need to. The only thing in life we know for certain is that everything is fluid and changing all the time. Show up for yourself and you will succeed. The best piece of advice I can give is to stay true to your goals and dreams. Ignore what society says we are supposed to do and be your own best cheerleader. Do it now because things change fast, and tomorrow may be too late.

If I learned anything from losing my career and both my parents in just a few years, it's that life will throw us curveballs, so we have to go for it and believe we can achieve anything. It's exciting when every day is a new day and the possibilities are endless!

About the author

Stephanie is a writer, artist, creative consultant, and optimist. She has been published in multiple areas, including three novels, children's books, graphic novels, shorts, and has worked in TV & film as an actress, artist, writer, script reader and script doctor.

She works with female writers in film, television and publishing by giving them actionable steps to help them create a prosperous, happy life and career they desire.

Website: www.stephaniebourbon.com
Facebook: www.facebook.com/JudanieBean
Email: stephanie@judaniebean.com

Szoey Freya Sølvelind

Hey, how are you? Feeling good? So far, I'm sure you've gained so much knowledge from the stories of all of the amazing ladies in this book - with your permission, I would love to give you mine as well. We good? Good!

My name is Szoey Freya Sølvelind - some call me Szoey, others call me Freya. In this chapter I will tell you the story of how I went from earning a "normal" decent pay in my company as a self employed Holistic Health Coach to completely changing my line of work - and without having an established audience or a webpage and with only 1,000 followers on my Instagram. I transformed my business to a multiple six figure business - just a few months after giving birth to my daughter. And, more importantly, if you stick around, I will give you some great pointers on how you can do the exact same thing as well. Sound good? Great!

Even though I did not know the steps along the way, I had

three keys to get me where I wanted to go: my intuition, fearlessness and a willingness to confront and transform all of the parts of my subconscious mind that were standing in the way of my success.

If the results I made sound completely bonkers to you and should it create a response of disbelief, don't worry. That doesn't mean you can't have it as well. Had I known the results I was going to make when my journey started, - I wouldn't have believed it either.

That is why I often say to my clients: your current self is not even able to understand what you can do, or how you are going to do it. Your current self has not yet taken the steps and the leaps of faith needed to expand in such a way. It sounds obvious but of course you can't comprehend how to do something before you learned how to do it. That's why we should always re-evaluate our goals along the way. The goals we set are just a reflection of what we believe to be possible at that time, in that moment. Goal setting should be fluid because you can do SO much more and WAY quicker than you actually think is possible. Believe me.

How it started

Before I had my big break in my company, I was already self employed as a Holistic Health Coach and had been for about three years. I was managing. I was paying my bills. I had, compared to many female entrepreneurs, created amazing results. I was proud of myself.

But it was stressful. What if my next course failed? What if I didn't hit my goals? What if my success ended abruptly? These thoughts were constantly hanging over me like a cloud. Usually, twice a year I would do a bigger course and in turn get a bigger income but each pay cheque was the last unless I was able to sell more. I had no guarantees of future sales or income. I had a tendency to earn a lot, then a little, then a lot. I was never quite confident or sure enough that I would hit the next big sale and if I didn't, I would be screwed financially.

I was doing the same courses over and over, but I was no longer passionate about them. I just didn't feel challenged anymore. I knew my courses worked well and they could sell. I thought the weightloss courses to be my bread and butter, so I kept with them, even though my passion for it had long gone. My lack of passion showed in my results. I was never able to hit my goal for a $30,000 launch, though it had been on my vision board for years and I kept making the same, mediocre results, even though I kept working on my planning, marketing, email streams and Facebook ads. Nothing made a difference.

I had known for at least a year, maybe even more, that I wanted to venture into mindset work, subconscious reprogramming, manifestation and shadow work. I wanted to do more. Do deeper work. I wanted to create massive financial expansion for myself and others. I wanted to teach other women how to live and create an income being self employed with good pay and less hours. I wanted to teach other women how to light their own flame, create their own fires and share their amazing knowledge with others.

I want women to have more power in society because I honestly and truly believe that women having more money will shift some of the values we hold on a societal level. That women having more money will prioritise mental health. Better bonds in our families. More time with our kids. Shorter and more flexible working hours - so less people burn out from stress and more people are allowed to thrive. All of these things are changes that NEED to happen in our society, in my opinion, because the way we are living now is so far from what is natural to us and what we need as people to be happy.

But, seeing as it was such a big jump from what I was doing at the time, I was scared. I was also pregnant and felt like it was simply not the time to make any rash decisions and change my field of work completely.

In the winter of 2019 and spring of 2020 I was heavily pregnant and as you can't get much financial help on maternity leave as a self employed lady in Denmark, I was really dreading it. I had decided to do one big launch before I was due to give birth. One last course. And I was bloody going to make my 30K! I had to. That would secure me while being on leave without having to stress about money…

I had fine tuned my programme and the content was excellent. I had even developed a new method to balance hormones in women whilst creating weightloss and I had created meal plans based upon body type according to hormone status, adrenal vitality, age and health. This had never been done in Denmark to my knowledge.

Rock bottom

A week before my launch, chaos struck. Someone dear to me who had once been a mentor, posted a programme very, very similar to the one I had made. As in, so similar, that some of the phrasing on their webpage was the exact same as on mine. Titles - the same. Description - the same. This new method that I had created - the exact same as I had teased on my webpage. Prices? Well, theirs were half the price that mine was.

I was angry. I was distraught. I was disappointed. And I lost my shit, quite frankly. I decided to give up on my course, since I didn't want to try and compete with them, as they had been in the game for longer. I acknowledged that I was not willing to fight to make the sales happen - my fire for holistic health had simply burned out. I simply decided to give it a rest and face the fact that I would be broke during my maternity leave. That my boyfriend would have to support me.

Around this time, COVID happened. A lot of my friends and family were in distress and I decided to write a blog post, recommending which herbal and vitamin supplements I knew to support immune health. The links on the blog were partnered, which meant I would earn around 2% of the amount the supplements costs, if anyone were to buy any. I didn't expect that to create any real income for me but as I was in the "sh*t" financially at this time, if I could earn a little coin that would've been very welcome. And once again, chaos hit. I was given a fine for recommending supplements to support your immune system. To my surprise, writing a blog post recommending herbal supplements is illegal in Denmark, if you are to earn anything from your recommendations. I had acted in good faith and had no idea that this is the law.

I was defeated. Just about to give birth and all of the money I had saved was going towards the fine. I was so sad and frustrated and in my frustration I wrote a post on facebook, expressing my sadness and disbelief of the situation and also questioning why suggesting Vitamin C supports your immune system should result in a fine. I thought that was something that was generally accepted knowledge.

This post went viral and got shared and shared and shared so much that a health debater wrote a blog post and a podcast episode about it. The content of this doesn't really matter but, needless to say, this blog and podcast made some statements from a somewhat skewed and untrue perspective.

Subsequently hundreds of his followers spammed me with messages saying everything from "I deserved what I got" to saying I was not fit to become a mother, to "I hope you get COVID and die". I was contacted by journalists who wanted me to defend why I had written the post. I received one of these calls on my due date. I was absolutely distraught.

I had always thought I would become famous but this was not exactly the kind of fame I thought I would receive.

There and then, I was finally COMPLETELY done. I was finally done being a Holistic Health Coach. I was scared about what the future would look like for me. I still wanted to be self employed but I wanted to do something that LIT ME UP. Something that lit my passion on fire.

A turning point

It seemed to me like fate was shouting at me, THIS IS NOT YOUR CALLING. THIS IS NOT YOUR WAY. Like, if someone copying my idea wasn't a hint enough for me, this sure was. I went completely off grid for a period of time. No social media. I had my baby (don't even get me started on my 90-something hours' birth, that could be a chapter in itself) and enjoyed life as a new mom. So, so much, but...

There was a flicker. A flicker of a flame, that had been turned on, in the midst of the storm. An, *"I am going to prove them."* An, *"I am done waiting for the life that I want"*. A fire. A flame. A fearlessness.

The last few months had been the most chaotic in my entire life. It felt like everything had completely burned down around me. The remainder of my old life didn't exist anymore and a new life had been born. A new identity had been born. I was a mom. A mom to a little girl who needed to see that everything was possible. I had gone through chaos and come out the other side and now there was nothing left that scared me.

At this time, my daughter was only just about two months old. But still, I had a voice inside of me telling me it was time. I didn't know why and I didn't know what it meant - but there it was. A silent whisper saying *"you are ready to open now."* So I set an intention and asked it to show me my next step.

The next day, a woman appeared on my Facebook. A business coach I had been following for a long time - a woman I had a feeling that I had business to do with, at some point. And there she was, with a video about business and intuition.

I watched it. Everything she said about how you can use your intuition to guide everything in your life and business echoed in me with a deep, inner knowing. A feeling of being home. A feeling of not understanding why, but knowing that it was my calling. That day, out of the blue, reached out to me and we had a conversation. And I just knew I had to work with her. I had thought I wanted to be on maternity leave for a year. This was not in my plans - it didn't make sense, but I had to work with her. It was my intuition, and it was speaking to me LOUDLY.

This woman was representing exactly what I wanted to be doing in my business and had the results that I wanted to create. She had just launched a course about creating quantum leaps in your business. I didn't know why, but I just knew that I had to do it. I asked my boyfriend, who said it was a bad idea.

So of course, I decided to do it.

The course cost just what I had in my account at that time and I had no plans to launch anything new. But I decided to trust my gut feeling and decided I didn't need to know why.

I didn't need to know how this made any sense, I just had to go with it. I had to listen to my intuition.

I started her course, and I set the intention to land the concept and idea for what I was going to do in my business. Within the span of two weeks, I had launched a course in using your intuition for guiding decisions in your business, reprogramming your subconscious mind, in manifestation and in shadow work. All of the things I was so goddamn passionate about and had been wanting to do for years. And in two weeks of signing up to that programme, I had earned my $30,000 that had been on my vision board for two years. I was teaching in something that was lighting my fire, and as I was doing so, the clients I had attracted started doing the same. They let themselves and their business be guided by intuition and their passion and so they created amazing results for themselves too.

In another month, I had earned $100,000. By the time I ended 2020, I had earned $330,000. And, more importantly, by not trying to think everything through. By not spending hours and hours perfecting a marketing plan and content but acting purely on passion and inspiration. I didn't work more than 10 hours a week. In actuality, instead of draining my energy and taking from me being a mother, working a couple of hours a day made me feel accomplished and like I was working towards something that our entire family would benefit from.

Precisely because I didn't spend all of this time analysing and overworking myself, I was so much more passionate when selling the course, so it was very easy to attract the women I wanted to work with. It felt like it was selling itself.

When I signed up with my coach, I decided to listen to my intuition. I took a leap of faith by investing all of the money I had on my account. I succeeded because I bloody well had to. I set the intention to follow every little step that my intuition told me to take. Even though every step along the way maybe didn't make sense in the physical dimension. I followed my passion, I stopped overthinking everything and I created a course that I was EXTREMELY passionate about. And I worked through any and all of my subconscious beliefs that were standing in the way of my success and transformed them.

In my courses I use an elaborate method and help my clients identify and transform these beliefs - but here is how you can start to use a more simple method yourself. I have inserted some examples from my own life but feel free to just use the method to get inspired.

1. Identify the area of your life that you want to change.

"I am not doing what I want in life and I am not creating the results I want to be making in my business."

2. Identify all of the underlying beliefs that are resulting in this reality.

"I think it will be difficult making money doing what I really want to be doing. I don't think it is time to do something new because I am a new mom. I am afraid to find out that I am not good at doing what I really want to be doing, so I will fail. And, essentially, I am afraid to be a failure and to not live my life's purpose and thus I will never really be happy."

3. Identify where you have learned those beliefs.

"All throughout school, my teachers told me I was no good. I have always been last in line. I was bullied. I am afraid to become a bad mother because I didn't have the childhood I wanted. I have learned that I am not lovable as I am and had to change to become accepted and loved."

4. Speak to those underlying beliefs from a space of your highest self, of love and intuition.

"My teachers told me I was no good because I didn't act how they expected and how they could control and comprehend. All along I was uniquely myself and although I learned to behave differently, I was in actuality a strong, independent little girl, who was loveable and creative. Feeling love and being loved is the reflection of loving yourself. When you love yourself, you act from intuition. When you love yourself, you are strong. When you love yourself, you don't have to change because you know that you are just how you are supposed to be. Love and confidence comes from within. You can be loved, confident and have the life you want when you are coming from a space of loving yourself. I love myself. I am enough. I am loved. I am following my dreams and being fearless because that is in alignment with who I really am. When I am in alignment with who it is I really am, I am happy. I love myself, when I am accepting myself as I am and following my dreams."

And repeat, repeat, repeat. Repeat until it sticks, and you actually believe it.

If I have a belief that I will be shunned or bullied, that I will fail and that I will not be loved doing what I really want to be doing, do you think I will do all in my power to create the life that I want? No. I will be making decisions and taking action that will result in me not succeeding because under my conscious want to create the life I want, I have subconscious, false beliefs working against me and sabotaging my results. Only when all parts of your mind and belief system, conscious and subconscious, are aligned with what you really want can you actually claim it.

Do you want to know how to create the results that I have made in the shortest span of time possible?

Be fearless.

Listen to your intuition. Listen to your gut feeling. Learn to trust that part of yourself that always JUST KNOWS. You do not need to know the how - all you need to know is the first step. And then the next step. And the next. If you get a calling to do something, get help from someone, to invest - DO IT. Stop stopping yourself and take action. Eliminate your excuses - they are only holding you back.

You do the work. You transform your beliefs. You repeat. Keep your eyes closed. Guide with your heart. Guide with your passion, your fire.

SHE DID IT

And take a leap of faith.

About the Author

Szoey Freya is a Psychic Business Coach & self-proclaimed FireWoman who teaches other female entrepreneurs how to earn a lot of money doing what they are passionately in love with. Being a FireWoman to Szoey means teaching other women who have an important mission in the world how to be successful – so that they can pass that knowledge on to the next women in line, and them to the next. Having more successful women in the world who know the importance of being led by love and intuition, Szoey thinks, will create a shift in our society for more flexibility and so much less stress, so many people are craving for.

She hopes to see passionate women all over the world being empower3ed to do what they love, have more freedom and work less hours, and yet still earn a more than amazing salary being self employed. Being a FireWoman means to lead the way and show that there is another way to live, and that way can be SO fulfilling, abundant and easy. In less than six months, Szoey built a 6-figure business doing what she loves, and she is here to tell you: YOU CAN TOO.

Website: szoeyfreya.com

Facebook: www.facebook.com/szoeyfreya

Email: hello@szoeyfreya.com

Vaida Cesnulyte

From a research scientist to a business owner

One of the things I love the most is successfully achieving my own goals. The other is seeing my first clients surpassing theirs. As I watch my clients achieving success it inevitably reminds me that I have been focused on goals and dreams since I was a little. I moved from my parent's home when I was 16 and lived with my grandmother for two years, where I finished secondary school. They were my best school years and grandma was my beloved friend and absolute rock.

Let's start at the beginning.

I haven't always been an entrepreneur. During my Bachelor Studies in Applied Mathematics, I had an increasing interest in understanding climate and its processes - especially the extreme events that causes the most damage to the surroundings. I wrote my final thesis on extreme precipitations and potential risks to nuclear power plants. I also worked as an engineer at the Lithuanian Energy Institute. I continued my research throughout my Masters studies with my main focus being extreme meteorological events - something I absolutely loved!

At the end of my Masters studies, I went through a painful break up with my partner of four and a half years. I found myself at a crossroads. I loved my work at the university but I had a clear understanding that if I wanted to pursue further studies in an environmental or climate change field, I needed to go to another country. After sending a couple of applications in France and Finland, I got the answer from Finland. After a few short weeks, I went for the interview in Helsinki. I remember how scared I was going by myself on a plane, finding my way to the hotel, finding the right trams to get to my interview on time. Thankfully, I got the position.

In May 2011, at the very end of graduating with an MSc in Applied Mathematics, I moved from Lithuania to Finland as I started a Doctoral studies (PhD) in Applied Physics and became a researcher in Finnish Meteorological Institute (FMI). I felt like my dream had come true.

You may wonder, *"Why Finland?"* It was something I'd

wondered myself.

Back 15 or more years ago, while my dad was still breeding Pyrenean Mastiffs, we went to Finland to a dog show in the winter. I found the whole trip incredibly boring. I told my dad on our way home that I wouldn't be coming back here again - there was nothing there but rocks, forest and snow. Little did I know back then that I'd be sat here today, writing this book, after ten years of living in - and loving - the country.

During that time I was a researcher. I published a manuscript and was a co-author for a couple of other scientific publications. I visited numerous scientific conferences in Europe and the USA to present my research and attended international schools. I was learning about the atmosphere, climate change and the human aspect to it.

Change

However, three and a half years into my research, I started to have mixed feelings about my future in academia and whether it was what I wanted my career to be. It bothered me as from the outside it looked like I had my whole future sorted out in the climate research field, but inside, I had my own inner fight about whether it was really the path I wanted to follow. It was painful and, for the most part, I kept it to myself. Before I could be sure that I wasn't just creating my own problems, I didn't want to tell anyone what I was thinking and going through. Now I see this is what most people do - they hide their feelings, thoughts and reasoning before they figure it out all on their own. I do not necessarily believe that this is the best way, however, back then, knowing how much everyone wanted my academic career for me, I could not share my feelings easily. It took me a whole year of thinking, evaluating and considering all the options for the future. I even took a month off before I made a decision to walk away from the scientific career.

Even though my love for the environment stays strong to this day, I wanted to move towards a corporate job or starting my own business. I wanted to make a different impact. It was the most difficult and challenging time of my life as many people from my close circle did not understand or approve of my decision to leave research work and a highly promising future career in academia. Additionally, I felt I was letting my family down as they'd put all their hopes, dreams and wishes for me on my career as a researcher. My dad once told me that I would have been the first PhD in the whole family, so it broke my heart thinking I was taking away the dream they wanted for me and for themselves.

I left PhD without having secured a corporate job. I left without having a clear plan, either. Every time I called my grandma, she would ask me if I was still using my math skills or if they had gone to waste now that I had quit PhD. I didn't know how to explain to her that math skills and analytical thinking aren't just something you use in a job. You use them all the time - in your life, as well when making career decisions, evaluating risks and planning your future. Analytical thinking is a way of life.

A PhD position can be a great milestone towards a further career in university or academia but it can also be a challenging road block if one decides to change one's career completely. That was me. People believe that if you arrive at that high level, you 100% know what you want and what your future is going to look like. This is true for most PhD students but definitely not for all. Now that I look back, I do not regret my decision. I'm happy I was a researcher, had that experience and had the courage to follow my intuition in the end. But after I made my decision, I met several other PhD students who felt the same way, but had not had the courage to leave nor the motivation to finish. I believe that is the worst place to be. Radical career change can be scary but it taught me two very important lessons: The first, that you won't know what's the right fit for you until you try it and, second, that getting stuck in indecision mode is far more self-damaging than trying and testing new opportunities, failing, then moving forward.

Next steps

After I left PhD, I worked as a Marketing Analyst in an online music education company and later on took on a job in car importing and digital marketing at a car sales company. I had also been building a Network Marketing business for six years on the side, which gave me robust digital marketing and branding skills that I used in my later work. But let's get back to CARS. This is where the fun in my life began! I have developed a huge passion for cars: driving, new models, exhibitions, importing cars, researching cars...anything and everything to do with them! There has never been a better combination for an introvert than to drive a car alone, long distance and with a good audiobook. Working in my now-fiance's car business allowed me to not only experience an entrepreneur's life in close proximity but also use my analytical thinking and maths knowledge to create tools, systems and strategies to make the business more effective. Good planning and goal setting skills are natural to me and

I thrived on the freedom of expression I had. I saw where things could be improved and systems could be created. This was the moment I started to think about my own consulting business. I saw real problems in real businesses that I could solve with my strong planning skills, analytical thinking and extended knowledge of online tools.

As a Type A personality myself – dominant, ambitious and a decisive doer - I am driven by goals and challenges. It is logical and simple for me to set any goal in my life, make a clear plan and work towards achieving it. This is how I have been able to accomplish countless small and big goals, from reading between 30 and 50 books a year for several years in a row and preparing and running a half-marathon, to finishing a Masters' Degree with honors, completing challenges and hitting sales quotas. It did not immediately occur to me that time management and productivity skills would be a valid foundation for my own consulting business. Usually, we tend to think that what is easy for us is easy for other people but that is not true.

In the early stages of starting my business, I did not know what exactly to offer. Back then, I was doing my own 90-day Facebook live video challenge and one of my videos led me to a business coach that helped me to create a consulting program. It was a starting point towards having my own business.

Taking the plunge

The hardest part in starting my business was the actual registration of the business. Not the paper work itself but the awakening realization that the comfort zone was over and from this time, my own and my business' wellbeing would depend on the effort I put in. That was scary. I also got approved for an entrepreneurs' grant and the moment I was informed of it, I freaked out. The panic was real, the fear was real, the understanding of the big change I had made was real. Five years after leaving research work, after several different jobs, time with no job, soul searching and uncertainty, I was about to start a new chapter as a business owner. Until then I did not notice how comfortable the comfort zone can truly be. No big responsibilities, no big effort, no big commitments, no big dreaming, either. I adjusted my life based on my income but did not work to adjust my income according to my dreams. When my company was registered and all paperwork was done, when there was no way back, I was confident and ready. Now there were two entrepreneurs under the same roof and I didn't know whether that was a good thing or more trouble.

I was quite fortunate to have my first clients right away and, as I have read tens of books on time management and productivity, I knew the objectives I want to cover and the most common problems entrepreneurs and small business owners face when it comes to getting their work done in the most effective way without burnout. So creating the actual program went rather fast and smoothly.

My first couple of clients had great results and achieved the goals they wanted to achieve in the time we worked together. And as much as the clear system I helped them to put in place had helped, they were action takers themselves from the very start! Ambitious, consistent, implementing everything right away. No wonder they had the results they had. Now I felt like I had it all figured out: my system is working, my first clients achieved the goals they wanted and I knew the exact problems they are facing. I was wrong. And a future client proved it.

This client had a busy, stressful life and lots on his plate: two businesses, a family, and studies. I was supporting him in implementing systems, tools, and tactics to help him get it all done and navigate his way through his busy life, but something wasn't working. I realized that the things that had worked for me and other clients did not work for him as well. The breakthrough came to me when I realized that I had tried to fix outer problems but I had not looked into the real, underlying causes of his lack of productivity.

When I looked back on my own journey, I could identify the same patterns, beliefs and challenges that stopped me from achieving some of my goals. While I was good at achieving most, some had been out of my reach. It bothered me. I had mental blocks, limiting beliefs and I was not confident enough. I didn't understand why the same person could have strong confidence in achieving certain goals whilst having a total fear of pursuing others. Sabotage, guilt, anger and fear were part of my life as well, so I could easily imagine how it must be for other people who pursue goals and never achieve them. I began researching the root causes and the mindset behind confident, productive people and the ways I could identify and measure them.

What I came to realize is that having clear goals, knowing how to plan your work, cleaning up your office or having all the skills on how to schedule your day may not lead to your desired productivity. Yes, they are no doubt important, but if we don't find what really motivates us, what core values we have, no matter how many tools, techniques, strategies and systems we learn, we will never be truly productive. If productivity is costing us our mental and physical health or making us unhappy,, it is not true productivity.

The steps

My research and studies led me to uncover several areas that are significant for understanding one's behavior and increasing personal productivity. Here are the three things that helped me immensely.

1. Do not stress about things you cannot control

I used to stress over things a lot that resulted in constant fatigue, irritation and anger. When I started to practise this skill, it changed my state of being and doing. Learn to identify the things you can control and those you cannot. In short, things we can control are our ATTITUDE, THOUGHTS, ACTIONS, and REACTIONS. Things we cannot control are everything else: the weather, other people's opinions, prestige, fame, money, body (we can get sick or be locked in jail against our will), reputation, spouse comments, reviews, traffic... the list is endless.

Starting today, for 30 days, every time you get angry

(whether it's because of a delayed or cancelled flight, you're stuck in traffic, a negative review, etc.), stop and yourself if you have control over this. If the answer is yes, work on changing it, if it's no, recognize it, acknowledge it, calm yourself down and use that time to do the next best thing you can do, for example, if you're stuck in traffic – pick a book or call a client whilst you wait, plane delayed. Mastering letting go of things we cannot control is the next step in finding peace, mental clarity and focus.

2. Know your core values in business and life

This was the key thing for me in realizing why I do not achieve particular goals year after year. When I made my values clear, it was obvious that the goals I was chasing were not important enough to me. I was chasing them because some else said they were awesome things to achieve. When I aligned my goals with my core values, it became easier to get up in the morning and do the work I needed to do each day. Knowing your core values helps you to navigate through tough decisions, say no to people, events and opportunities, save yourself from feeling guilty, build self-confidence, eliminate a need to compare yourself to others, build self-accountability and bring purpose and meaning in life and business.

Google the phrase, *"list of 100 personal core values."* Go through that list and write down the ones that speak to you. Aim for no more than 15. There are no right or wrong core values. If it's important for you, it's worth adding. You are most likely already living your life by the majority of those values but not aware of them. Out of the 15, check if you can group some (e.g. if you have knowledge and growth, they can be grouped together, then you can just pick the one that you like more). Ultimately, you want to have a maximum of between five and seven core values and every time you have a hard time making a decision or each time you map your year and plan goals, look at your core values and check if they are in alignment. You will never have a hard time deciding what to do, saying no, accepting or declining offers. if you use your core values as a rock solid guide that everything has to pass through.

3. **Own your day**

For many years, especially after I walked away from my PhD, I was either worried about what would happen in the future or was upset with events in the past. I was not living in the present. It cost me a great deal of enjoyment and appreciation by not living in a moment. As much as you want to think a year, month, week ahead, this exact day is all we have. Tomorrow is not promised to anybody. Owning your day means taking control of your day, being proactive and not reactive. Your one, five or 10 year goals come down to how well you control one day at the time – today.

Each morning scan your day ahead and imagine what could go wrong, the absolute worst scenario and how you would respond to it. This way you will be less stressed, calmer and more thoughtful, also, you will be better prepared for the day ahead. For example, you have a job interview coming today. You sent the CV by email a few days ago and are ready for your meeting. Imagine that a virus got into the company's servers and the interviewer or CEO cannot get to your CV and therefore hasn't read it. This quick worst-case-scenario thinking prompts you to print a CV and carry it with you, just in case. Now you are in control, calm, prepared and ready.

These are only three simple but powerful steps you can take to greatly improve your productivity, self-confidence and level of self-responsibility towards achieving your short and long-term goals. Part of my 2021 business goal is to create an Optimal Productivity Assessment –a well-structured questionnaire that helps to identify the key causes behind unproductive performance. It evaluates areas I mentioned above like self-accountability, responsibility, self-confidence, stress and anxiety levels, motivation, effectiveness and energy levels, to name a few. The core root causes of unproductive performance and sabotaging mindset. It will be a cooperation with skilled human behavior experts, statisticians, programmers and web developers. My goal is to work on helping entrepreneurs and business owners create a strong foundation and solid habits that lead to life-long results in business and their personal lives. It all comes down to personal effectiveness and personal productivity. Life that is driven by a clear purpose and run by strong core values can be truly rewarding, fulfilling and successful in all areas.

If my grandma could fully understand the work I am doing and the tools I am working to create, she would probably be very delighted knowing I am using all my Math knowledge, analytical thinking and research skills to bring the best quality service and methods to my clients so they can go out into the world and crush their personal and professional goals while having strong reasoning, sharp focus and mental clarity.

About the author

Vaida Cesnulyte is a productivity and time management expert and an online business strategist. She has over seven years of experience in the field of goal setting, planning, mindset, online business management tools and energy management. She helps entrepreneurs and small business owners to put systems in place to make it easier to run their businesses and create more time freedom. Vaida moved from her home country of Lithuania to Finland, where she lives with her fiancé, Jani. She has BSc and MSc degrees in Applied Mathematics and worked as a research scientist in a climate change field. When she is not working, she loves reading books, horseback riding, hiking and driving cars.

Website: www.creaplan.fi
Facebook: www.facebook.com/vaida.cesnulyte/
LinkedIn: www.linkedin.com/in/vaidacesnulyte/
Email: vaida@creaplan.fi

Made in United States
North Haven, CT
24 July 2022

21743150R00169